FONDUE AND HOT

Joanna White

BRISTOL PUBLISHING ENTERPRISES
San Leandro, California

A **nitty gritty**® Cookbook

Printed in the United States of America.

ISBN: 1-55867-254-0

Cover design: Frank J. Paredes
Cover photography: John A. Benson
Food stylist: Susan De Vaty
Illustrations: Pamela Johnson

CONTENTS

1   Introduction

    1   Fondue Do's and Don't's

    3   Fondue Equipment

    5   Cooking Temperatures

6   Cheese Fondues

23   Hot Dips

43   Oil and Broth Fondues

60   Cooking Broths

73   Dipping Sauces

99   Dessert Fondues

119   Index

INTRODUCTION

Fondue is making a big comeback. It is a great vehicle for intimate, easy entertaining. The preparation is done in advance so the hosts can relax, be with their guests and let them do the cooking.

Fondue is traditionally one of three things: cheese fondue comes from the classic Swiss dish; fondue *bourguignonne* refers to cooking meat in hot oil and dipping it in one of a variety of sauces; and chocolate fondue is a concoction of melted chocolate and sometimes liqueur into which cake or fruit is dipped. Today's fondue brings more choices, such as cooking in a flavorful, healthy broth instead of oil. Included in this book are recipes for a variety of cheese fondues, hot dips, recipes for cooking in oil or broth, assorted cooking broths, dipping sauces and fabulous dessert fondues.

A typical fondue party would consist of a starter course with a cheese fondue, a creative green salad, an entrée course, which includes several types of meat and vegetables cooked in a broth or oil accompanied by dipping sauces and, of course, a dessert fondue. Happy dunking!

FONDUE DO'S AND DON'T'S

1. Do not experiment on guests—always try the recipes first.
2. If using several electrical fondues, heating plates, coffee makers, etc., plug in all the units to make sure you do not blow a fuse. (Trust me—I learned this from experience!)
3. Avoid using cheese rinds in fondues or the flavor will be too sharp.
4. Have salt and pepper (preferably a pepper mill) on the table, but caution the guests to season their food after it is cooked. Salt will cause oil to splatter, herbs will burn in the oil, and the cooking broth (or oil) may become over-seasoned.
5. I like to make labels when there is a large variety of dipping sauces—this prevents confusion and the need to repeat the information during the party.
6. Place a large platter under a fondue pot that is filled with oil to avoid ruining your tablecloth.
7. A nice accompaniment to the meal is small bowls of fresh herbs that were ingredients in the marinade, for your guests to sprinkle on their cooked meats.
8. Try not to make too many varieties of fondues at a party. As host you will end up constantly trying to monitor the flames, water levels and texture of the fondue instead of spending time with your guests.

9. If fondue becomes too thick while warming, thin down with a little hot liquid used in the original recipe (i.e., hot cream, milk, wine, liqueur, etc.).

10. Use oil that can handle high heats, such as pure vegetable oil or peanut oil. It is a good idea to have a paper plate or a plate lined with paper towels to absorb the excess oil.

11. Inform your guests about fondue etiquette: do not eat from the fondue fork since you will be returning it to the pot; also, the heated fork can burn your lips.

12. Do not exceed 6 guests per table. Duplicate the fondue arrangement at other tables to avoid overcrowding the pots.

13. Each guest should have a plate, knife, fork, spoon, several fondue forks or bamboo skewers and lots of napkins!

14. Traditional European fondue is always served with wine, prosciutto and pepper. If you lose your morsel of meat in the pot, you are supposed to kiss your neighbor.

FONDUE EQUIPMENT

1. Fuel sources are denatured alcohol, solid-fuel burners, electric elements or votive candles. When heating oil or cooking broth, I generally prefer to use the

first three sources, but votive candles work best when keeping fondue mixtures warm.

2. Thick ceramic pots work well with cheese and dessert fondues that require low to moderate heat.

3. Metal fondue pots that can take high heat are best used for broth and oil fondues. Buy the models that have a smaller rim than base, to prevent oil splashes. Avoid using thin metal pots for cheese and dessert fondues because the mixtures will burn.

4. Porcelain-glazed cast iron pots and pots with water bath jackets are best for all kinds of fondues.

5. Electric fondue pots with thermostatic controls work best for maintaining consistent heat. I prefer the models that have a separate vessel and heating element for easy cleaning. Note: Make sure the electrical cord is placed out of the walking area so it cannot be pulled off the table.

6. If you don't have enough fondue pots for your party, improvise with double boilers over portable burners.

7. Forks for fondues have long tines and two or three points. The handles are marked with different colors so your guests won't mix up their forks. I like to use wood-handled forks to prevent burning hands when hot oil heats the

metal tines.

8. Dipping sauces are generally served in small bowls surrounding the fondue pot. Sometimes I serve the sauces on a turnstile so people can easily reach the food.

9. Long bamboo skewers are also used to spear foods. Soak the skewers in water for 20 minutes so there is less chance of the wood burning in hot oil.

COOKING TEMPERATURES

When working with electric fondue sets use the following settings:

Cheese fondues   170°F or 85°C or setting from 3 to 4

Oil fondues   350°F or 180°C or setting number 6

Broth fondues   Start with 350°F or 180°C or setting number 6. After it comes to a boil, reduce to 200°F or 100°C or setting numbers 4 to 5.

Dessert fondues   150°F or 70°C or setting numbers 2 to 3

Note: If you don't have a thermostat control, use a deep fat fryer thermometer to monitor the oil temperature.

CHEESE FONDUES

7	Dutch Cheese Fondue
8	Caramelized Onion Fondue
9	Smoked Cheese Fondue
10	Green Chile Fondue
11	Fiesta Cheese Fondue
12	Mediterranean Fondue
13	Creamy Brie Cheese
14	Danish Cheese and Bacon Fondue
15	Nonalcoholic Cheese Fondue
16	Creamy Shrimp Fondue
17	Chicken and Cheese Fondue
18	Swiss Cheese and Egg Fondue
19	Stilton Cheese Fondue
20	Easy Cheddar Beef Fondue
21	Buttermilk Fondue
22	Chili Fondue

DUTCH CHEESE FONDUE

Mix Dutch Gouda and Edam together for a more complex flavor. Serve with a mixture of breads such as French, pumpernickel and rye. This also goes well with assorted vegetables, especially mushrooms. Caraway seeds are sometimes added for a unique flavor, but try a little sample and see if it appeals to you first.

2 cups dry white wine	2 tbs. kirsch liqueur
1 tsp. chopped garlic, or more to taste	1/4 tsp. nutmeg
1 lb. Dutch Gouda or Edam cheese, grated	fresh ground pepper to taste
	dash Tabasco Sauce
1 tbs. cornstarch	dash Worcestershire sauce

Pour wine into a 2-quart fondue pot or enamel casserole dish. Bring wine to a boil over high heat and add garlic. Let wine and garlic boil for 2 minutes; remove garlic with a slotted spoon. Lower heat to a simmer. Stirring constantly with a fork, add cheese a handful at a time, allowing cheese to melt before adding another handful. In a small bowl, stir together cornstarch and liqueur. When all cheese is added and fondue is creamy and smooth, stir in cornstarch mixture along with nutmeg, pepper, Tabasco Sauce and Worcestershire sauce. Taste and adjust seasonings. Adjust heat so fondue is just barely simmering.

CARAMELIZED ONION FONDUE

Caramelizing onions gives them a sweet flavor that adds a new twist to Swiss fondue. Serve with an assortment of bread cubes and parboiled baby potatoes.

1 tbs. butter
1 tbs. olive oil
1½ cups thinly sliced onions
2 tsp. sugar
salt and pepper to taste

2 cups dry white wine
1 lb. Gruyère cheese, shredded
2½ tbs. flour
¼ tsp. ground nutmeg
fresh ground pepper to taste

Heat butter and oil in a skillet over medium-high heat. Add onions and sauté for 3 minutes. Reduce heat to low and sprinkle wilted onions with sugar, salt and pepper.

Cook on low heat, stirring occasionally until onions are caramelized, about 15 minutes; transfer to a small bowl. In a fondue pot or enamel pot, heat wine to simmering on medium-low heat. Add ½ of the caramelized onions. Toss cheese and flour together until cheese is well coated. Add cheese mixture by handfuls to simmering wine, stirring with a fork until cheese is melted. Continue to add remaining cheese by handfuls, stirring until smooth each time. Add nutmeg and pepper to taste. Garnish fondue with remaining caramelized onions and keep warm over low heat.

SMOKED CHEESE FONDUE

Serve with cooked kielbasa sausage, bockwurst, bratwurst or even frankfurters. If you like a little texture, garnish the fondue with cooked, crumbled bacon. Rye bread goes especially well with this fondue.

1 cup beer
¼ cup coarsely chopped onion
3 cups shredded smoked cheese
1 cup shredded Emmentaler cheese

1 tbs. cornstarch
¼ cup cream
1 tsp. German or Dijon mustard

Heat beer in a fondue pot until bubbly. Add onion and cook for 3 minutes. Remove onion with a slotted spoon and gradually stir in cheeses until melted. In a small bowl, combine cornstarch and cream until smooth, and stir into cheese mixture. Stir in mustard and keep mixture warm over low heat.

GREEN CHILE FONDUE

Serve with bread cubes or cooked meats and fish such as chicken, sausage or shrimp, and your favorite selection of fresh vegetables. This recipe can also be used as an appetizer hot dip served with tortilla chips.

1 cup whole milk
$\frac{1}{2}$ lb. Jack cheese, shredded
$\frac{1}{2}$ lb. sharp cheddar cheese, shredded
2 tbs. cornstarch
1 tsp. ground cumin
1 can (4 oz.) diced green chiles
$\frac{1}{2}$ cup cooked, crumbled bacon for garnish, optional

In a heavy saucepan, heat milk until just ready to bubble. In a bowl, mix together Jack cheese, cheddar cheese, cornstarch and cumin. Add cheese mixture a handful at a time to milk, stirring until fondue is smooth and all cheese is melted. Transfer melted cheese mixture to a fondue pot and keep warm over low heat. If desired, garnish with cooked, crumbled bacon.

FIESTA CHEESE FONDUE

Here is cheddar cheese fondue with the flavor of Mexican spices, salsa and jalapeños, if desired. Serve with crisp tortilla chips, bread cubes, rolled tortillas, cooked meats, crackers or even potato chips. I like to use chunky salsa for extra texture.

1 1/2 cups beer
1 tsp. minced garlic
1 lb. cheddar cheese
1 tbs. cornstarch
2 tbs. water
1/2 cup salsa, mild or hot

1 tsp. chili powder
1/2 tsp. ground cumin
1–3 tsp. jalapeño chiles, minced and
   seeded, to taste

In a saucepan, heat beer until it begins to foam, and add garlic. Simmer for 1 minute. Add cheese a handful at a time, stirring constantly until all cheese is melted. Mix cornstarch with water and stir into cheese mixture until mixture thickens slightly. Add salsa, chili powder, cumin and jalapeños, if desired. Taste, adjust seasonings and add more salsa if desired. Transfer to a fondue pot and keep warm over low heat.

MEDITERRANEAN FONDUE

Blue cheese gives a nice sharp edge to this fondue. Serve with chunks of salami, assorted bread cubes, large pitted olives, or pieces of cooked beef and chicken.

2 cups milk
2 tsp. minced garlic
3 cups shredded mozzarella cheese
3/4 cup shredded Parmesan cheese (prefer Asiago)
12 oz. blue cheese, crumbled
1 1/2 tbs. cornstarch
6 tbs. dry white wine

Heat milk and garlic in a fondue pot until bubbly. Add cheeses a handful at a time, stirring until cheese melts before adding more cheese. Mix cornstarch with wine and stir into cheese mixture until mixture thickens. Reduce heat to low to keep warm.

CREAMY BRIE CHEESE

This creamy fondue goes well with fruit (especially apple) and bread. I've also used commercially prepared puff pastry, cut into strips for easy dipping and baked according to package instructions.

½ cup dry white wine
¾ cup half-and-half
½–1 tsp. minced garlic, to taste
12 oz. Brie or Camembert cheese
4 tsp. cornstarch
¼ cup apple brandy

Heat wine with half-and-half in a fondue pot until bubbly; add garlic. Cut rind from cheese and discard. Cut cheese into small pieces and add to wine mixture a few pieces at a time, stirring until cheese is melted. Repeat until all cheese is melted. Mix cornstarch with brandy and add to cheese mixture. Stir until thickened. Reduce heat to low to keep warm.

DANISH CHEESE AND BACON FONDUE

This fondue is traditionally served with small sweet and sour gherkin pickles and rye bread. Another idea for dunkers is 1-inch pieces of cooked sausage, frank-furters or bockwurst.

$^1/_2$ lb. lean bacon, finely diced
1 tbs. butter, optional
$^1/_2$ cup chopped onion
1 tbs. flour
1 cup beer
2 cups shredded Danish Samsoe or Emmentaler cheese
2 cups shredded Havarti cheese

In a large saucepan, cook bacon on medium-high heat until crisp. Add butter to pan if less than $1^1/_2$ tbs. bacon fat remains. Stir in onion and sauté until wilted. Stir in flour until absorbed; add beer and stir until mixture is thickened. Add cheeses by the handful, stirring until cheese melts; repeat until all cheese is melted. Transfer mixture to a fondue pot and keep warm over low heat.

NONALCOHOLIC CHEESE FONDUE

This fondue is made with apple juice or cider instead of wine or beer. Serve with sliced apples, fruit, or an assortment of breads. Using apple juice instead of beer makes a sweeter cheese mixture. Increase the amount of lemon juice if you wish to decrease the sweetness.

1 cup apple cider
2 tsp. lemon juice
1 tbs. finely chopped onion
3 cups shredded medium cheddar cheese
1 tbs. cornstarch
2/3 tsp. dry mustard powder
1/4 cup apple cider
1/4 tsp. white pepper

Heat apple cider, lemon juice and onions in a fondue pot until bubbly. Add cheese by handfuls, stirring until melted. Repeat until all cheese is melted. Mix cornstarch and mustard in 1/4 cup apple cider. Add to cheese mixture; stir until mixture thickens. Add white pepper, taste and adjust seasonings. Reduce heat to low to keep warm.

CREAMY SHRIMP FONDUE

Servings: 4-6

This easy recipe gives the impression you spent a lot of time preparing. Use cooked shrimp, prawns, fish cubes, or cubes of French bread for dipping.

1 1/4 cups milk
2 cans (10 3/4 oz. each) cream of shrimp soup
1/2 tsp. minced garlic
4 cups grated Swiss cheese
1/2 cup vermouth or sherry
1/4 tsp. white pepper, or to taste
1/4 tsp. paprika

Heat milk in a fondue pot. Add soup and garlic; stir until smooth. When soup mixture begins to bubble, add Swiss cheese by handfuls, stirring until cheese melts. Repeat until all cheese is melted. Stir in vermouth, pepper and paprika. Taste and adjust seasonings. Keep warm over low heat.

CHICKEN AND CHEESE FONDUE

Turkey can be substituted for chicken in this recipe. Serve with bread cubes, vegetables, and if desired, unmarinated cooked chicken cubes.

1 chicken, about 2½ lb.
3 cups canned chicken broth
5 green onions
1 tsp. minced garlic
⅔ tsp. dried tarragon

1 cup grated Gruyère cheese
1 tbs. flour
¼ cup brandy or Chablis wine
3 egg yolks
¾ cup cream

Cut chicken into several pieces. Place in a large saucepan with chicken broth, green onions, garlic and tarragon. Bring to a boil, reduce heat, cover and simmer for 1 hour, or until chicken is tender. Remove skin and bones and cut chicken into small pieces. Strain stock through a sieve and place ½ cup in a food processor workbowl or blender container. Add chicken and puree until smooth. In a saucepan, bring 1½ cups broth to a boil and add cheese, stirring until cheese is melted. Mix flour with brandy or wine; stir into cheese mixture. In a bowl, beat egg yolks with cream. Pour a little of the hot cheese mixture into the egg yolk mixture; pour egg yolk mixture into cheese mixture, and stir until mixture thickens. Add pureed chicken, taste and adjust seasonings. Transfer mixture to a fondue pot and keep warm over low heat.

SWISS CHEESE AND EGG FONDUE

Servings: 4

This is a creamier version of the typical Swiss fondue. Serve with assorted breads, vegetables and cooked poultry.

1 1/3 cups Chablis wine
1/2 lb. Swiss cheese, grated
1 1/2 tsp. cornstarch
1/3 cup kirsch liqueur
4 egg yolks
2/3 cup cream
salt and white pepper to taste

Heat wine to boiling in a fondue pot. Add Swiss cheese by handfuls, stirring well until cheese melts. Mix cornstarch with kirsch and add to cheese mixture, stirring well. In a bowl, beat eggs yolks with cream. Pour a little of the cheese mixture into the egg mixture, and then pour egg mixture into fondue pot. Stir until mixture thickens, about 5 minutes.

Add salt and white pepper, taste and adjust seasonings. Keep warm over low heat.

STILTON CHEESE FONDUE

Stilton is a popular cheese in England, usually served with fruit for dessert. This is a gourmet fondue that goes well with assorted breads, vegetables and cooked poultry.

1/4 cup butter
1 cup chopped onion
1/2 cup chopped carrots
1/2 cup chopped celery
1 bay leaf
1/3 cup flour

3 cups hot chicken broth
3 cups half-and-half
1/2 lb. Stilton cheese, crumbled
1 tsp. English mustard
pepper to taste

In a large saucepan, heat butter. Add onion, carrots, celery and bay leaf; cover and cook on low heat for 5 minutes. Add flour, stir and cook on medium heat for 2 minutes. Add chicken broth and cook on medium-high heat for 10 minutes. Strain mixture through a sieve and discard solids. Stir in half-and-half and mix well. Slowly add cheese in small quantities; stir until smooth. Add mustard and pepper, taste and adjust seasonings. Transfer mixture to a fondue pot and keep warm over low heat.

EASY CHEDDAR BEEF FONDUE

This nonalcoholic version of fondue can be made in minutes. The chopped beef is optional and any cooked beef, sausage, pork or even chicken can be substituted. Serve with cubes of bread, vegetables or unmarinated, cooked meats.

2 cans (10¾ oz. each) cream of mushroom soup
1 lb. sharp cheddar cheese, grated
¼ cup flour
1 tbs. Worcestershire sauce
2 cups chopped dried beef or chopped smoked ham
2 green onions, finely chopped

In a large saucepan, heat soup on medium heat until it bubbles. Mix cheese with flour. Add cheese by handfuls to soup, stirring until smooth each time. Add Worcestershire sauce, chopped beef and green onions. Stir to combine and transfer mixture to a fondue pot. Keep warm over low heat.

BUTTERMILK FONDUE

Buttermilk gives a little tang to this easy fondue. Serve with assorted bread cubes (especially rye bread), frankfurter chunks, vegetables or cubes of ham.

1 1/2 cups buttermilk
1/2 cup beer
1 lb. Muenster cheese, shredded
2 tbs. cornstarch
2 tsp. Dijon mustard
1/4 tsp. white pepper, or more to taste

In a saucepan, heat buttermilk and beer on medium heat until it bubbles. Mixture will look curdled but will smooth out. Mix cheese and cornstarch together. Add by handfuls to buttermilk mixture, stirring constantly until cheese melts; repeat until all cheese is incorporated. Stir in mustard and white pepper, taste and adjust seasonings. Transfer mixture to a fondue pot and keep warm over low heat.

CHILI FONDUE

This one is a favorite of children because of the familiar taste of processed cheese. Serve with bread cubes, large tortilla chips, rolled tortillas, breadsticks, cooked, unmarinated beef or chicken and assorted vegetables.

1 tbs. olive oil
1 1/4 cups chopped onion
1 can (28 oz.) diced tomatoes, drained
1 can (4 oz.) chopped green chiles
1/2 tsp. minced garlic
1 1/2 lb. processed cheese, cubed
1/2 lb. mild cheddar cheese, shredded
dash Tabasco Sauce

In a saucepan, heat olive oil on medium heat, add onion and cook until wilted. Add tomatoes, chiles and garlic; cook for 5 minutes. Add cheese a handful at a time and stir until cheese is melted; repeat until all cheese is melted. Stir in Tabasco Sauce and transfer mixture to a fondue pot. Keep warm over low heat.

HOT DIPS

24	Marsala Tomato Dip
25	Crab Dip
26	Sausage Mushroom Dip
27	Corned Beef Dip
28	Hot Barbecue Dip
29	Hot Clam Dip
30	Basil Marinara Dip
31	Savory Blackberry Dip
32	Red Curry Dip
33	Italian Anchovy Dip
34	Apricot Sauce
35	Hot Shrimp and Mushroom Dip
36	Feta Cheese and Cilantro Dip
37	Green Chile and Artichoke Dip
38	Hot Bean Dip
39	Gorgonzola Dip
40	Hot Spinach Dip
41	Beef and Bean Dip
42	Pecan Sour Cream Dip

MARSALA TOMATO DIP

This dip is excellent with large pasta noodles or ravioli. Serve shredded Parmesan alongside for dipping, or sprinkle a little on top for garnish. Other possibilities are cooked gnocchi dumplings, cooked meatballs or cubes of French bread.

1 can (29 oz.) chopped tomatoes, with juice
1/2 onion, chopped
1 tsp. sugar
1 cup chicken broth
1/2 cup dry white wine

1/4 cup Marsala wine
1 tsp. minced garlic
1/2 tsp. dried thyme
1/2 tsp. dried oregano
salt and pepper to taste
1/4 cup butter

Place tomatoes, onion, sugar, broth, wine, Marsala, garlic, herbs, salt and pepper in a heavy saucepan and simmer for 40 minutes. Transfer to a food processor workbowl or blender container and puree until smooth. Pour sauce into a fondue pot and stir in butter. Keep warm over low heat.

CRAB DIP

Serve this gourmet dip with crackers, bread and assorted vegetables.

1 cup chicken broth
2 tbs. dry sherry
1 tsp. salt
2 tbs. vegetable oil
1 tsp. sesame oil
1 pinch white pepper
2 tsp. cornstarch
2 tbs. cold water
1–2 tbs. chopped cilantro, to taste
2 cups crabmeat

In a saucepan, bring chicken broth to a boil. Add sherry, salt, oil, sesame oil and white pepper. Mix cornstarch with cold water and stir into heated mixture; cook until mixture becomes clear and thickens slightly. Stir in cilantro and crabmeat; taste and adjust seasonings. Transfer mixture to a fondue pot and keep warm over low heat.

SAUSAGE MUSHROOM DIP

This flavorful combination is popular with adults and children. Serve with bread cubes, fresh mushrooms or cooked sausage. Use the leftover dip as a sauce to serve over cooked eggs.

1 lb. pork sausage
1/2 lb. mushrooms, thinly sliced
1 tsp. lemon juice
3/4 cup chopped onion
1 cup sour cream
2 tbs. flour

1 cup milk
1 tbs. Worcestershire sauce
1 tsp. soy sauce
1 tsp. paprika
salt and pepper to taste, optional

In a skillet, cook sausage until brown. Remove and drain meat on paper towels. Sprinkle mushrooms with lemon juice and cook with onion in remaining fat in skillet until slightly wilted. Pour off excess fat from skillet and add cooked sausage back to the pan. In a bowl, stir together sour cream, flour, milk, Worcestershire sauce, soy sauce and paprika. Stir into sausage mixture and cook on medium-low heat until mixture thickens. Taste and add salt and pepper if desired. Transfer sauce to a fondue pot and keep warm over low heat.

CORNED BEEF DIP

Serve this German-style dip with cubes of rye, pumpernickel and/or French bread. Or cut rectangles of toasted cheese bread for dipping.

½ cup sweet red wine
1 cup shredded Swiss cheese
1 cup sauerkraut, drained
1 tsp. Dijon or grainy mustard
1 tsp. dried dill weed
1 tbs. finely minced onion

1–2 tsp. honey, to taste
¼ cup mayonnaise
salt to taste
dash lemon pepper
6 oz. corned beef

In a saucepan, cook wine to boiling. Add cheese, stirring until melted. Add sauerkraut, mustard, dill weed, onion, honey, mayonnaise, salt and lemon pepper; stir to mix. Shred corned beef and stir into mixture. Taste and adjust seasonings. Transfer to a fondue pot and keep warm over low heat.

HOT BARBECUE DIP

This is an all-time favorite, especially for cooked pork, beef, chicken and lamb. If you like a spicier dip, add more Tabasco Sauce or minced jalapeños to taste.

2 cups ketchup
1/2 cup cider vinegar
1/2 cup brown sugar or molasses
1 cup finely minced onion
1 tsp. dry mustard
2 tbs. lemon juice
dash Tabasco Sauce, or more to taste
salt to taste

In a large saucepan, stir all ingredients together and cook on medium-low heat for 15 minutes. Taste and adjust seasonings. Transfer mixture to a fondue pot and keep warm over low heat.

HOT CLAM DIP

Serve with assorted bread cubes, cooked shrimp or fish or large cooked pasta shells. Consider serving leftover clam dip over cooked pasta, with an extra sprinkling of Parmesan cheese.

2 tbs. olive oil
1 cup chopped onion
2 cups clam juice
1 tbs. minced garlic
1 1/2 cups dry white wine
1/2 cup chopped fresh parsley

1–1 1/2 tsp. red pepper flakes, to taste
3/4 tsp. salt, or to taste
1/4 cup butter
2 tbs. lemon juice
1 1/2 cups chopped clams
1 cup shredded Parmesan cheese

In a skillet, heat oil on medium-high heat and cook onion until soft. Add clam juice, garlic, wine and parsley and cook until liquid is reduced by half. Add red pepper flakes, salt, if desired, and butter; stir until butter is melted. Transfer mixture to a fondue pot. Just before serving, stir in lemon juice, clams and Parmesan. Keep warm over low heat.

BASIL MARINARA DIP

Breadsticks work very well with this great dip. Use any unmarinated, cooked meat for dipping: steak cubes, chicken pieces, lamb cubes or prawns.

2 tbs. olive oil
3 tbs. butter
1 onion, chopped
2 1/2 cups canned tomatoes, with juice
1 1/2 tsp. minced garlic
1/2 cup Marsala wine
1/2 cup chopped fresh parsley

1/2 tsp. salt, or more to taste
1 tsp. pepper
1/2 tsp. nutmeg, optional
1 tbs. sugar
1/4 cup chopped fresh basil, or 1 tbs.
   dried basil

Heat oil and butter over medium-high heat in a heavy saucepan. Cook onion until wilted, about 3 to 4 minutes. Finely chop tomatoes and add to onion with garlic, wine, parsley, salt, pepper, nutmeg and basil. Cook on medium heat for 1/2 hour. Taste and adjust seasoning. Transfer mixture to a fondue pot and keep warm over low heat.

SAVORY BLACKBERRY DIP

This unique and flavorful dip goes well with cooked duck breast, chicken and cubes of salmon.

1½ cups fresh or frozen blackberries
⅓ cup sugar, or more to taste
½ cup water
2 tbs. lemon juice, or more to taste
6 oz. Chinese hoisin sauce

Place berries, sugar and water in a saucepan; cook on medium heat for 20 minutes. Remove from heat and press mixture through a sieve to remove seeds. Place in a fondue pot and stir in lemon juice and hoisin sauce. Taste and adjust seasonings by adding either more sugar or lemon juice. Keep warm over low heat.

RED CURRY DIP

This spicy, tomato-based dip goes well with assorted fresh or roasted vegetables, cooked poultry, beef and lamb. Start off with a small amount of curry powder and keep adding more until you reach the amount of spice you desire.

$1/4$ cup olive oil
2 tbs. butter
2 onions, finely chopped
$1–1 1/2$ tbs. minced garlic, or more to
   taste
2 tbs. curry powder, or to taste

16 oz. tomato sauce
6 tbs. balsamic vinegar
2 tsp. salt
2 tbs. sugar
1 pinch cayenne pepper

Heat olive oil and butter in a saucepan and cook on medium heat until onions are wilted. Add garlic and curry powder and cook on medium-low heat for 5 minutes. Add tomato sauce, vinegar, salt, sugar and cayenne pepper; cook for 5 minutes longer. Taste and adjust seasonings. Transfer to a fondue pot and keep warm over low heat.

ITALIAN ANCHOVY DIP

A favorite in Italy—serve this with a large assortment of fresh vegetables or bread cubes. This dip can also be used to dunk cooked meats or cubes of cooked white fish.

1 1/2 cups olive oil
6 tbs. butter
1 tbs. minced garlic
6-8 anchovies, mashed
1/4–1/2 tsp. black pepper, to taste
salt to taste, optional

In a saucepan, heat oil and butter until butter just melts. Add garlic and cook for just a few moments (do not brown garlic). Add mashed anchovies and pepper, mixing well. Taste and determine if you wish to add salt or more anchovies. Transfer mixture to a fondue pot and keep warm over low heat.

APRICOT SAUCE

This is a quick and easy sauce that goes well with fish, pork and wild game. Serve this sauce either hot or cold.

1¾ cups apricot jam
1¾ tbs. light soy sauce
3 tbs. minced green onion
1¼ tbs. lime juice
dash Tabasco Sauce
salt and pepper to taste

If apricot jam is lumpy, process with a blender or food processor until smooth. Place jam, soy sauce, onion, lime juice and Tabasco Sauce in a saucepan and cook on medium heat until warm. Taste and add salt and pepper if desired. Transfer mixture to a fondue pot and keep warm over low heat.

HOT SHRIMP AND MUSHROOM DIP

This creamy dip has nice eye-appeal. Serve with French bread cubes, crackers, assorted vegetables, cooked prawns and fish.

1 tbs. butter
1 tbs. olive oil
$1/2$ lb. mushrooms, thinly sliced
1 tsp. lemon juice
2 cans ($10^3/4$ oz. each) cream of shrimp soup
$3/4$ lb. small shrimp
$1/4$ cup grated Parmesan cheese
2 tsp. Worcestershire sauce
2 tbs. finely chopped fresh parsley
pepper to taste, optional

In a large saucepan, melt butter; add olive oil, mushrooms and lemon juice. Cook on medium heat until mushrooms are soft. Add soup, shrimp, cheese, Worcestershire sauce, parsley, and pepper if desired. Stir to combine; taste and adjust seasonings. Transfer to a fondue pot and keep warm over low heat.

FETA CHEESE AND CILANTRO DIP

Makes 2 cups

Here's a quick dip that goes well with assorted bread cubes, crackers, cooked poultry and large Greek olives. Sometimes I add ½ cup chopped Greek olives to the recipe.

1½ cups cream
6 tbs. finely chopped cilantro leaves
½ lb. feta cheese, crumbled
pepper to taste, optional

In a fondue pot, heat cream and cilantro until mixture bubbles. Add feta cheese in small amounts and stir until creamy. Taste and determine if you wish to add pepper. Keep warm over low heat.

GREEN CHILE AND ARTICHOKE DIP

This is a quick recipe that is very popular with guests. Serve with assorted cubes of bread, crackers, breadsticks and vegetables. I've also used marinated, well-drained artichokes. They make the dip a little oilier, but more flavorful.

1 cup chopped, unmarinated artichokes
1 can (4 oz.) diced green chiles
¾ cup chopped black olives
1 cup grated Parmesan cheese
1 cup mayonnaise
½ cup grated cheddar cheese

In a saucepan, heat artichokes, chiles, olives, Parmesan and mayonnaise on medium heat until just heated through. Add cheddar cheese and stir until melted. Transfer to a fondue pot and keep warm over low heat.

HOT BEAN DIP

Serve this with rolled-up tortillas, tortilla chips, bread cubes, cooked frank-furters, unmarinated cooked beef, pork or chicken and assorted vegetables.

1 can (30 oz.) pork and beans
½ cup grated cheddar cheese
1 tsp. minced garlic
1 tsp. chili powder
½ tsp. salt, or more to taste
2 tsp. Worcestershire sauce
½ tsp. Liquid Smoke
dash cayenne pepper or Tabasco Sauce

Place all ingredients in a food processor workbowl or blender container and process into a puree. Transfer mixture to a fondue pot. Heat on medium heat until creamy. Taste and adjust seasonings; reduce heat to low.

GORGONZOLA DIP

Gorgonzola is a semi-soft cheese that resembles blue cheese but is a little drier. It has a piquant flavor, and is generally used in salads or served with fruit for dessert. Try this creamy dip with vegetables, beef, chicken or cooked onion rings.

3 tbs. butter
2 tbs. minced onion
2 tsp. minced garlic
1 cup beef stock

1 cup red wine (Cabernet Sauvignon, Merlot or Zinfandel)
2 cups crème fraiche*
½ lb. Gorgonzola cheese, crumbled
pepper to taste

In a skillet, heat butter on medium and cook onion until wilted. Add stock and wine; cook on medium-high heat until reduced by half. Stir in crème fraiche and again reduce by half. Mix in Gorgonzola and pepper and stir until smooth. Taste and adjust seasonings. If mixture is too lumpy, place in a food processor workbowl or blender container and puree until smooth. Transfer mixture to a fondue pot and keep warm over low heat.

* Crème fraiche is now readily available in large-chain grocery stores, found in the refrigerator case near the sour cream. Sour cream can be substituted for crème fraiche, but you must be careful not to allow the mixture to get too hot.

HOT SPINACH DIP

This pungent dip goes well with assorted vegetables, bread cubes and cooked chicken. If you like it really hot, add more jalapeños and some of the seeds.

2 tbs. olive oil
1–2 jalapeño chiles, seeded and
  chopped, to taste
1 cup chopped onions
1 can (14 1/2 oz.) diced tomatoes,
  drained
1 can (4 oz.) mild or hot green chiles

1 pkg. (10 oz.) frozen chopped spinach
1 1/2 tbs. balsamic or other red wine
  vinegar
1 pkg. (8 oz.) cream cheese, softened
1 cup half-and-half
2 1/2 cups grated Monterey Jack cheese
salt and pepper to taste

In a large saucepan, heat oil on medium-high heat. Cook jalapeños and onions until wilted. Add tomatoes and green chiles; cook for 1 to 2 minutes. Defrost spinach and squeeze dry. Add spinach, vinegar and cream cheese; stir until cream cheese melts. Stir in half-and-half and Jack cheese gradually, until cheese is melted. Taste and determine if you wish to add salt and pepper. Transfer mixture to a fondue pot and keep warm over low heat.

BEEF AND BEAN DIP

Mexican food is always a great hit at casual parties. Serve with tortilla chips, bread cubes, rolled tortillas, and cooked frankfurters, beef, pork or poultry.

1 lb. lean ground beef
1 cup chopped onion
$1/2$ cup ketchup
4 tsp. chili powder
1 tsp. salt
2 cups kidney beans, undrained
1 cup grated sharp cheddar cheese
$1/2$ cup stuffed green olives, sliced
$1/2$ tsp. Tabasco Sauce, or more to taste

Brown beef and onions in a skillet on medium-high heat. Stir in ketchup, chili powder and salt. With a food processor or blender, process beans with liquid until pureed; add to beef mixture. Stir in cheddar cheese until melted; stir in olives and Tabasco Sauce. Taste and determine if you wish to add more Tabasco Sauce or salt. Transfer mixture to a fondue pot and keep warm over low heat.

PECAN SOUR CREAM DIP

This is a popular Southern dip: it goes well with breadsticks, crackers, apples and vegetables.

2 pkg. (8 oz. each) cream cheese, softened
1 cup sour cream
¼ cup milk
1 cup chopped dried beef
4 tsp. minced green onions
1 tsp. garlic salt
1 tbs. butter
1 cup chopped pecans

In a bowl, mix cream cheese, sour cream and milk until smooth. Add beef, green onions, and garlic salt; stir well. In a small skillet, heat butter on medium-high heat. Cook pecans, stirring constantly until browned. Add cream cheese mixture to toasted pecans; stir until heated through. Transfer mixture to a fondue pot and keep warm over very low heat.

OIL AND BROTH FONDUES

44 Asian Chicken

45 Marinated Lamb

46 Quick and Easy Beef Fondue

47 Fried Cheese

48 Shrimp and Vegetable Tempura

49 Tender Chicken Slices

50 Prawn Balls

51 Ginger Beef

52 Marinated Steak

53 Double Dip Meatballs

54 Battered Fish

55 Spicy Chicken Tenders

56 Merlot Lamb

57 Cherry-Marinated Chicken

58 Coconut Chicken

59 Beer-Marinated Beef

ASIAN CHICKEN

For this dish, chicken is marinated in a wonderful sesame oil and soy mixture. Serve with Daikon Radish Dipping Sauce, *page 83,* Garlic Lemon Dipping Sauce, *page 89, and/or* Parsley Dipping Sauce, *page 80.*

2 lb. boned, skinned chicken breast
    meat
1 cup chopped onion
1 1/2 tsp. mashed garlic
10 tbs. soy sauce
2 tbs. sugar

1/4 cup sesame oil
1/2 tsp. ground pepper
1 tbs. cornstarch
vegetable oil to barely cover chicken
toasted sesame seeds for garnish,
    optional

Cut chicken into cubes or strips and place in a bowl. Add onion, garlic, soy sauce, sugar, sesame oil, pepper and cornstarch; stir to mix. Pour enough vegetable oil to barely cover chicken; cover and refrigerate for at least 1 hour, or overnight. Drain chicken well and reserve liquid. Either sprinkle drained chicken with sesame seeds before serving or, heat reserved marinade, add sesame seeds and serve as a dipping sauce with meat. Cook chicken in hot oil or hot broth for about 2 minutes.

MARINATED LAMB

Marinated lamb can be cooked in oil or broth. For an alternative, make small skewers with fresh pineapple wedges and 1-inch squares of red and green bell peppers. Serve with Cilantro Peanut Sauce, *page 81,* Curry Mayonnaise, *page 87, and/or* Garlic Lemon Dipping Sauce, *page 89.*

2 lb. lamb shoulder
1/4 cup lime juice
1/4 cup olive oil
1 cup finely chopped onion
2 tsp. minced garlic

1/4–1/2 tsp. Tabasco Sauce, to taste
2 tsp. curry powder
3 tsp. ground ginger
4 tsp. turmeric
2 tsp. salt

Cut meat into 1-inch cubes and set aside. In a bowl, mix together lime juice, olive oil, onion, garlic, Tabasco Sauce, curry, ginger, turmeric and salt. Pour marinade over meat and stir until meat is coated thoroughly. Cover and refrigerate overnight. Cook in hot oil or broth of choice for about 1 1/2 minutes.

QUICK AND EASY BEEF FONDUE

Servings: 4

The more tender the meat, the more your guests will remember this dish. Serve with Sour Cream Horseradish Sauce, *page 79,* Dijon Mustard Sauce, *page 78,* Béarnaise Sauce, *page 77,* Curry Mayonnaise, *page 87, and/or* Green Goddess Dipping Sauce, *page 75.*

$\frac{1}{2}$ cup olive oil
3 tbs. balsamic or other red wine vinegar
1 tsp. salt
$\frac{1}{2}$ tsp. ground pepper
1 tsp. dried marjoram
$\frac{1}{2}$ cup finely chopped onion
2 lb. tender boneless beef (tenderloin, sirloin steak or chuck steak)

In a large bowl, combine olive oil, vinegar, salt, pepper, marjoram and onion. Remove any visible fat from beef and cut into 1-inch cubes. Pour marinade over meat, cover and refrigerate for at least 1 hour, or overnight. Cook in hot oil or hot beef broth for about 1$\frac{1}{2}$ minutes.

FRIED CHEESE

Servings: 6-8

This recipe can be served as an appetizer or main course. For a change, use seasoned breadcrumbs for a stronger flavor. Serve with Blueberry Dipping Sauce, *page 94, or* Cherry Dipping Sauce, *page 97, as an accompaniment.*

12 oz. Camembert, Gorgonzola, Cambazola or Brie cheese, chilled for easy cutting
1/2 cup flour seasoned with salt and pepper
2 eggs, beaten
1 cup dry breadcrumbs or Japanese panko breadcrumbs

Cut chilled cheese into 1-inch cubes; if desired cheese can be rolled into balls. Dredge cheese pieces in seasoned flour; dip in beaten eggs and finally in the breadcrumbs. Repeat to ensure a crunchy crust. Place on a plate and chill until ready to use. Cook in hot oil until brown.

Note: Cheese will tend to ooze out if fried too long.

SHRIMP AND VEGETABLE TEMPURA

Servings: 8

I've listed my favorite tempura vegetables, but any combination of vegetables will work. Serve with Soy Dipping Sauce, *page 82, or* Daikon Radish Dipping Sauce, *page 83: some even like it with* Sweet and Sour Sauce, *page 86.*

3 large eggs, cold
2/3 cup water, ice cold
1 cup flour
32 medium-sized uncooked prawns,
    peeled and cleaned
2-3 onions, cut into rings
4 carrots, cut into slices diagonally

1/2 lb. mushrooms
1–2 yams or sweet potatoes, peeled
    and sliced
1/2 lb. pea pods, strings and ends
    removed
1/2 head cauliflower, cut into florets

In a bowl, combine egg whites and yolks until just barely mixed. Stir in water and then flour. Do not overmix. Slit prawns halfway down inner curve without cutting through (butterfly cut). Dip prawns and vegetables in batter and cook in 375° oil until crisp, about 2 minutes. Serve immediately.

Note: To reduce greasiness, allow fried food to drain on paper towels for 1/2 minute before serving.

TENDER CHICKEN SLICES

This is an excellent method of tenderizing poultry. Serve with Dijon Mustard Sauce, *page 78,* Daikon Radish Dipping Sauce, *page 83,* Sweet and Sour Sauce, *page 86,* Béarnaise Sauce, *page 77,* Garlic Lemon Dipping Sauce, *page 89, and/or* Green Goddess Dipping Sauce, *page 75.*

1 lb. boneless, skinless chicken breast meat
1/2 tsp. salt
1 tbs. dry sherry
6 tbs. flour
1 tsp. baking powder
2 eggs, beaten
1/4 cup water
salt and pepper to taste

Pound chicken breast meat with a wooden mallet or rolling pin to tenderize. Cut into 2-inch by 1/2-inch thick slices and place in a bowl with salt and sherry. In a separate bowl, mix together flour, baking powder, eggs, water, salt and pepper, until a smooth paste is formed. If batter appears too thick, add 1 tbs. water. Dip chicken in batter and cook in 375° oil until chicken is golden, about 1 1/2 to 2 minutes.

PRAWN BALLS

Panko breadcrumbs are Japanese-style crumbs that give fried foods a special crunchy texture. Serve with Soy Dipping Sauce, *page 82,* Sweet and Sour Sauce, *page 86, and/or* Plum Sauce, *page 91.*

1½ lb. uncooked prawns, peeled and deveined
1 can (8 oz.) water chestnuts, drained and finely chopped
3 tbs. butter
1 egg white, beaten
1½ tbs. dry sherry

1 tbs. grated fresh ginger
2 tbs. minced green onions
1 tbs. chopped fresh cilantro, optional
2 tsp. salt
2 tbs. cornstarch
panko breadcrumbs for coating

With a food processor or blender, gently pulse prawns until finely chopped but not pureed. Transfer chopped prawns to a bowl. Add water chestnuts, butter, egg white, sherry, ginger, green onions, cilantro, salt and cornstarch. Stir well and form into balls (you may need to wet your hands with a little water to help form the balls). Carefully coat balls in panko breadcrumbs and cook in 375° oil until golden brown, about 1½ to 2 minutes.

GINGER BEEF

Marinated beef has much more flavor than plain beef. Cook this marinated beef in hot oil or beef stock. Serve with Parsley Dipping Sauce, *page 80,* Soy Dipping Sauce, *page 82,* Garlic Lemon Dipping Sauce, *page 89, or* Sour Cream Cilantro Dipping Sauce, *page 93.*

1/2 cup finely minced onion
1 tsp. minced garlic
1 tsp. turmeric
1 tbs. minced fresh ginger, or 1 tsp. ginger powder
1/2 tsp. chili powder
1/2 tsp. salt
1 1/2 lb. beef tenderloin or sirloin

In a large, shallow bowl, combine onion, garlic, turmeric, ginger, chili powder and salt for marinade. Cut meat into large, paper-thin slices and mix with marinade. Cover and refrigerate for at least 3 hours. Cook meat in hot oil or beef broth for about 1 1/2 minutes.

MARINATED STEAK

This recipe can also be used to marinate chicken, lamb or wild game. Serve with Dijon Mustard Sauce, *page 78,* Sour Cream Horseradish Sauce, *page 79,* Green Mayonnaise, *page 90, and/or* Danish Dill Dipping Sauce, *page 92.*

$\frac{1}{2}$ cup lemon juice	1 tsp. Dijon mustard
$\frac{1}{3}$ cup olive oil	1 tsp. Worcestershire sauce
1 tbs. grated lemon zest	$1\frac{1}{2}$ tsp. salt
2 tbs. finely minced onion	$\frac{1}{8}$ tsp. pepper
1 tsp. minced garlic	$1\frac{1}{2}$ lb. steak
$1\frac{1}{2}$ tbs. sugar	

Place all ingredients except steak in a blender or food processor workbowl and process until well combined. Cut steak into 1-inch chunks and place in a shallow glass dish. Pour marinade over steak pieces. Cover and marinate for at least 3 hours, or overnight in the refrigerator. Cook in hot oil or beef broth for about $1\frac{1}{2}$ minutes.

DOUBLE DIP MEATBALLS

Makes 24-30

For this recipe, meatballs are cooked in oil and dipped in a favorite cheese fondue. Ground chicken or turkey can be substituted for ground beef. You can also serve these with Remoulade Sauce, *page 88,* Parsley Dipping Sauce, *page 80,* Sweet and Sour Sauce, *page 86, or* Sour Cream Cilantro Dipping Sauce, *page 93.*

2 lb. ground sirloin or chuck
1 cup grated Parmesan cheese
1/2 cup finely chopped fresh parsley
1 1/2 tsp. minced garlic
2 cups Italian breadcrumbs

2 large eggs
1 tsp. salt
1/2 tsp. pepper
1 tsp. dried basil, oregano, rosemary or
  marjoram, optional

In a large bowl, mix all ingredients together except 1 cup of the breadcrumbs. Make a small patty and cook in a skillet. Taste and determine if you wish to adjust seasonings or add one of the optional herbs. Roll meat mixture into 1 1/2-inch balls and dredge in remaining breadcrumbs. Meatballs can be dipped into cooking oil with a slotted spoon and cooked until brown and crisp, about 2 to 2 1/2 minutes. Drain cooked meatballs on paper towels, and dip them in cheese fondue.

Note: If you wish to use a fork to cook the meatballs in oil, first place meatballs on a baking pan and bake at 400° for 10 minutes to make them firm.

BATTERED FISH

This is an excellent batter for seafood, as well as onion rings, slices of potato and mushrooms. Serve with Béarnaise Sauce, *page 77,* Danish Dill Dipping Sauce, *page 92,* Sour Cream Cilantro Dipping Sauce, *page 93,* Soy Dipping Sauce, *page 82,* Sweet and Sour Sauce, *page 86, or* Green Goddess Dipping Sauce, *page 75.*

¾ cup flour
1 tsp. salt
¼–½ tsp. cayenne pepper or Tabasco
   Sauce, to taste
⅓ tsp. baking soda
pepper to taste
1 cup plus 2 tbs. buttermilk

1 large egg
2 tbs. club soda
1 tbs. grated lemon zest
1½ lb. white fish (cod, flounder, or
   sole) or seafood of choice
seasoned flour for dredging (flour
   mixed with salt and pepper)

In a bowl, combine flour, salt, cayenne, baking soda and pepper. In a separate bowl, combine buttermilk, egg, soda, and lemon zest until well mixed. Combine and let stand for 20 minutes before using. Cut fish into 1-inch cubes, dredge pieces in seasoned flour, and dip in buttermilk batter. Cook in 360° oil for about 2 minutes. Drain on paper towels before serving.

SPICY CHICKEN TENDERS

For this recipe, instead of marinating the chicken, dredge it in spicy seasoned flour and cook in hot oil. Serve with Dijon Mustard Sauce, *page 78,* Parsley Dipping Sauce, *page 80,* Sweet and Sour Sauce, *page 86,* Green Goddess Dipping Sauce, *page 75, and/or* Curry Mayonnaise, *page 87.*

6 boneless chicken breast halves
2 cups flour
1 1/2 tsp. paprika
1 tsp. Old Bay seasoning
1/2 tsp. dried thyme
1/2 tsp. dried basil
1/2 tsp. dried oregano
1/2 tsp. garlic powder
1/2 tsp. pepper
1/4 tsp. cayenne pepper
2 large eggs
2 tbs. water

Remove skin from chicken, cut each breast into 4 long slices, and cut each slice in half. In a bowl, mix together flour, paprika, Old Bay seasoning, thyme, basil, oregano, garlic powder, pepper and cayenne. In a separate bowl, beat eggs and water together.

Dip chicken pieces in egg mixture, and then in flour mixture. Lay pieces out on a platter and refrigerate until ready to serve. Cook in 375° hot oil for about 2 minutes or until brown and crisp.

MERLOT LAMB

This marinade can also be used for wild game. Serve with Cilantro Mustard Dipping Sauce, *page 85,* Parsley Dipping Sauce, *page 80,* Dijon Mustard Sauce, *page 78, and/or* Sour Cream Horseradish Sauce, *page 79.*

1 cup Merlot wine
1/3 cup olive oil
1 tsp. salt
1 tbs. minced garlic
3/4 tsp. pepper
1 1/2 tsp. dried rosemary
2 1/2 lb. boneless lamb

In a nonaluminum bowl, mix together wine, olive oil, salt, garlic, pepper and rosemary. Cut lamb into 1-inch cubes. Mix lamb with marinade, cover and refrigerate overnight.

Cook in hot oil or broth for about 1 1/2 to 2 minutes.

CHERRY-MARINATED CHICKEN

The secret ingredient in this marinade is Campari, an Italian aperitif. The marinade can also be used for beef, veal and pork. Serve with Garlic Lemon Dipping Sauce, *page 89,* Béarnaise Sauce, *page 77, and/or* Sour Cream Cilantro Dipping Sauce, *page 93.*

¼ cup olive oil
1 cup finely chopped onion
1½ tbs. minced garlic, or more to taste
6 tbs. lemon juice
1 tsp. salt
½ tsp. pepper
1½ tsp. sugar

¾ cup Campari
½ cup Chablis or other dry white wine
juice from 1 can (16 oz.) dark sweet
    cherries
½ tsp. dried thyme
¼ cup finely chopped fresh parsley
1½ lb. boneless, skinless chicken
    breast meat

In a saucepan, heat oil on medium and add onion. Cook until onion is wilted; add garlic, lemon juice, salt, pepper, sugar, Campari, wine and cherry juice. Cook for about 7 to 8 minutes; remove from heat and stir in thyme and parsley. Cool marinade to room temperature. Cut chicken meat into 1-inch chunks, place in marinade, cover and refrigerate for 3 hours. Remove chicken from marinade, skewer with forks and cook in hot oil or cooking broth for about 2½ minutes.

COCONUT CHICKEN

This flavorful coconut marinade has a little punch of heat from the jalapeños. Serve with Yogurt Chutney Dipping Sauce, *page 84,* Sweet and Sour Sauce, *page 86,* Curry Mayonnaise, *page 87, and/or* Sour Cream Cilantro Dipping Sauce, *page 93.*

1/2–1 jalapeño chile, to taste
1 can (14 oz.) coconut milk
1 1/2 tbs. curry powder
2/3 cup brown sugar, packed
1/3 cup finely chopped fresh cilantro
1 tbs. chopped fresh mint
1/2 tsp. salt
2 1/2 lb. boneless, skinless chicken breast meat

Carefully cut jalapeño open, remove seeds and finely mince. In a bowl, combine coconut milk, curry powder, brown sugar, cilantro, mint and salt; mix well. Cut chicken breasts into 1-inch chunks and place in bowl with marinade. Stir well to coat chicken, cover and refrigerate overnight. Remove chicken from marinade about 1 hour before serving. Cook chicken in hot oil for about 2 to 2 1/2 minutes.

BEER-MARINATED BEEF

Beer is a natural tenderizer and adds a distinct flavor. Serve with Dijon Mustard Sauce, *page 78,* Sour Cream Horseradish Sauce, *page 79,* Remoulade Sauce, *page 88,* Parsley Dipping Sauce, *page 80,* Cilantro Peanut Sauce, *page 81, and/or* Garlic Lemon Dipping Sauce, *page 89.*

1 can beer (avoid dark ales)
3 tbs. apple cider vinegar
1/4 cup dark brown sugar
1 1/2 tsp. minced garlic
1/2 tsp. salt
1/4 tsp. pepper
2 tbs. finely chopped fresh parsley
1 pinch dried marjoram
2 lb. flank or other steak

Mix beer, vinegar, sugar, garlic, salt, pepper, parsley and marjoram in a glass baking dish. Cut steak into 1-inch cubes and stir into marinade. Cover and refrigerate for several hours. Cook in hot oil or broth for 1 1/2 to 2 minutes.

COOKING BROTHS

61 Oriental Cooking Broth
62 Coq au Vin Cooking Broth
63 Court Bouillon
64 Fish Stock
65 Beef Stock
66 Wine Cooking Broth
67 Sukiyaki Broth
68 Sukiyaki Dinner
69 Saffron Broth
70 Madeira Broth
71 Mushroom Broth
72 French Onion Broth

ORIENTAL COOKING BROTH

Makes 6 cups

This broth is especially good for cooking chicken, fish and vegetables. A small amount of soy sauce can be added for a more intense flavor.

6 cups chicken broth, fresh or canned
1/2 cup chopped scallions
6 slices fresh ginger
3 cloves garlic, peeled
1 hot red chile, optional
few drops sesame oil

Place all ingredients in a saucepan or directly into a fondue pot. Bring mixture to a boil, reduce heat and simmer for 15 minutes. Remove ginger, garlic and red chile before serving.

COQ AU VIN COOKING BROTH

Makes 4 cups

Use this wine and vegetable broth as an excellent alternative to cooking in oil. It is great for cooking raw meats, poultry, fish and vegetables. Substituting Burgundy for white wine gives a more robust flavor.

4 cups dry white wine
½ cup chopped carrots
½ cup chopped celery
½ cup chopped onion
½ cup chopped leeks
1 cup sliced mushrooms
3 cloves garlic, peeled

12 white peppercorns
2 bay leaves
handful fresh parsley stalks
sprig fresh thyme
sprig fresh rosemary
1 pinch sugar
salt to taste

Place wine, carrots, celery, onion, leeks, mushrooms, garlic and peppercorns in a large saucepan. Wrap bay leaves, parsley, thyme and rosemary in cheesecloth and tie with string. Add herbs to saucepan and bring to a boil, reduce heat to medium and cook for 30 minutes. Add sugar, taste and determine if you wish to add salt. Discard vegetables and herb bundle. Sieve mixture through a strainer and pour liquid into a fondue pot. Heat mixture to a boil for cooking.

COURT BOUILLON

This aromatic liquid is excellent for cooking fish, shellfish, poultry and vegetables. Court bouillon is used to cook more delicate foods, where the flavor of the vegetables can be absorbed into the food.

2 quarts water
1 cup dry white wine
2 carrots, diced
1 medium onion, diced
4 shallots or 3 green onions, diced
2 stalks celery, diced

2 tsp. black peppercorns
1 bay leaf
handful fresh parsley stalks
sprig fresh thyme
salt to taste

Place water, wine, carrots, onion, shallots, celery, peppercorns and bay leaf in a large saucepan. Wrap parsley and thyme, in cheesecloth and tie with string. Place in the saucepan and bring mixture to a boil. Reduce heat to medium and cook for 25 minutes. Discard vegetables and herb bundle. Strain mixture through a sieve and transfer to a fondue pot. Heat mixture to a boil for cooking.

FISH STOCK

This stock is good for dunking pieces of cod, halibut, salmon, sole, prawns and lobster. It can also be used for cooking vegetables.

1 lb. white fish bones (sole, flounder, or cod)*
1 quart water
⅓ cup dry white wine
½ onion, coarsely chopped
2 lemon slices

6 peppercorns
1 bay leaf
handful fresh parsley stalks
sprig fresh thyme
salt to taste, optional

*Note: Use fish bones from white fish and avoid oily fish bones such as herring, mackerel and salmon. You can use fish heads, but remove eyes and gills first.

Wash fish bones and chop into pieces. Place in a large saucepan with water, wine, onion, lemon slices, peppercorns, bay leaf, parsley stalks and thyme. Slowly bring to a boil, reduce heat and allow to simmer for 15 to 20 minutes, but no longer, or stock will become bitter. Skim any froth from the surface while stock is simmering. Strain stock through a sieve. Taste and determine if you wish to add salt. Transfer sieved mixture to a fondue pot and bring to a boil to cook seafood and vegetables.

BEEF STOCK

This stock is a perfect choice for all kinds of beef, lamb, veal and pork entrées. A small amount of red wine gives it extra flavor. Use only the stalks of parsley; the leaves will give the stock a green color.

1 lb. beef soup bones and/or beef
   brisket
1 quart water
$\frac{1}{2}$ onion
4 whole cloves
1 stalk celery with leaves, chopped

1 carrot, coarsely chopped
1 bay leaf
small handful fresh parsley stalks
8-10 peppercorns
sprig fresh thyme
salt to taste

Place bones and brisket in a baking pan and bake at 400° for 1 hour, until bones are well browned on both sides. Place bones and water in a large saucepan. Stud onion with cloves and add to saucepan with celery, carrot, bay leaf, parsley stalks, peppercorns and thyme. Slowly bring to a boil and skim off any froth that floats to the surface. Lower heat, cover and simmer for 3 to 4 hours. Discard solids, strain, and add salt to taste. Transfer stock to a fondue pot and boil pieces of raw meat in mixture.

WINE COOKING BROTH

This broth works well for poultry and fish as well as assorted vegetables. Another possibility is to use this broth as a dipping sauce for toasted bread cubes.

3 cups dry white wine
1 1/2 cups canned or homemade chicken broth
2 tsp. minced fresh ginger, or 1 tsp. ground ginger
1 tbs. chopped green onions
1 tsp. dried tarragon
salt and pepper to taste

Place wine, chicken broth, ginger and onions in a fondue pot; heat until almost boiling. Add salt and pepper to taste. Keep broth at a simmer for cooking.

SUKIYAKI BROTH

Sukiyaki beef and onions are partially cooked in oil, dipped in beaten egg and cooked in the sukiyaki broth along with the other vegetables. If you wish to make a more traditional version, add squares of tofu, sliced bamboo shoots and a bunch of spinach.

2 cups water
1 cup beef or chicken broth
$1/2$ cup sake rice wine or dry sherry
$2/3$ cup light soy sauce
1 tsp. sugar
2 slices fresh ginger

Place water, broth, sake, soy sauce, sugar and ginger in a fondue pot and cook for 10 minutes to infuse ginger flavor.

SUKIYAKI DINNER

Beef, vegetables and noodles create an entire meal. Guests can finish cooking at the table.

1½ lb. sirloin, cut into large paper-thin slices
1 bunch green onions, cut into 1½-inch slices on the diagonal
1 lb. mushrooms, cut in half if large
½ lb. napa cabbage, cut into large chunks
½ lb. noodles (udon, rice noodles, or spaghetti)
4 carrots, cut into matchstick strips
6 eggs, beaten

Cook meat and onions in hot oil for ½ minute and arrange on a platter along with cabbage. Cook noodles according to package instructions. Cook carrots in water until tender-crisp, about 5 minutes; blanch in cold water and arrange on platter with noodles. Place a bowl of beaten egg by each guest. Dip meat into beaten egg and cook in broth for 1 minute. Cook remaining vegetables in broth until tender. Dip noodles in sauce to warm.

SAFFRON BROTH

This is a wonderful broth in which to cook seafood—white fish, scallops, lobster and prawns. It also works well for vegetables, especially potatoes.

1 tbs. olive oil
1 cup chopped onion
1 cup chopped fennel
2 tsp. minced garlic
5 cups chicken broth

1 cup dry white wine
1 tbs. tomato paste
1/2 tsp. dried thyme
scant 1/8 tsp. powdered saffron
salt to taste, optional

Heat olive oil on medium in a large saucepan and stir in onion, fennel and garlic. Cook for about 5 minutes, until onion is wilted. Add chicken broth, wine, tomato paste, thyme and saffron and bring to a boil. Reduce heat and simmer for 15 minutes. Taste and determine if you want to add salt. Leave vegetables in broth, or if you like a clear broth, strain mixture through a sieve. Transfer broth to a fondue pot; keep at a low boil to cook raw fish and vegetables.

MADEIRA BROTH

This clarified beef broth has an intense flavor. Use it to cook cubes of beef, veal, lamb or wild game along with an assortment of vegetables.

4 cups canned beef stock
3 egg whites
1 leek, cut into thin slices
½ lb. lean ground beef
1 large carrot, cut into thin slices

1 stalk celery, cut into thin slices
2 medium tomatoes, diced
⅓ cup Madeira wine, or more to taste
salt and pepper to taste

Heat beef stock on medium heat in a large saucepan. In a bowl, beat egg whites with a whisk until foamy. Add leek, beef, carrot, celery, and tomatoes to egg whites and slowly stir into heated stock. Cook stock over medium heat, whisking constantly until mixture begins to bubble and look milky. Continue to cook for 2 minutes longer. Reduce heat to low and cook uncovered for 45 minutes: do not stir. Remove from heat and strain through a sieve lined with cheesecloth; discard solids. Add Madeira to stock and season with salt and pepper. Transfer stock to a fondue pot.

MUSHROOM BROTH

This very quick broth can be made vegetarian by using vegetable broth in place of chicken broth. This broth can be used to cook all of the proteins including beef, veal, poultry, seafood and vegetables.

³/₄ lb. mushrooms, finely chopped
6 cups chicken broth
6 tbs. dry sherry
pepper to taste

In a large saucepan, bring mushrooms and chicken broth to a boil. Reduce heat and simmer for 15 minutes. Strain mixture through a sieve and add sherry. Taste and add pepper if desired. Transfer mixture to a fondue pot and use in place of oil for cooking meats and vegetables.

FRENCH ONION BROTH

Try this quick version of an old-time favorite pureed to serve as a cooking broth for beef, poultry, pork and vegetables. Another possibility would be to serve this with toasted cheese bread cut into cubes. Chicken or vegetable broth can be substituted for the beef broth.

$^1/_4$ cup butter
$2^1/_2$ cups thinly sliced onions
2 tsp. sugar
6 cups beef or chicken broth
dash dry sherry
$^1/_4$ tsp. pepper, or to taste
salt to taste, optional

Heat butter in a skillet. Cook onions with sugar on medium heat, stirring frequently, until well browned (caramelized). This will take about 15 to 20 minutes. Add broth, sherry and pepper to onion mixture; cover and cook on medium-low for 30 to 40 minutes. Taste and adjust seasonings. Pour mixture into a food processor workbowl and blend until onions are pureed. Transfer mixture to a fondue pot. Use to cook raw meats and vegetables.

DIPPING SAUCES

75   Green Goddess Dipping Sauce
76   Cucumber Sauce
77   Béarnaise Sauce
78   Dijon Mustard Sauce
79   Sour Cream Horseradish Sauce
80   Parsley Dipping Sauce
81   Cilantro Peanut Sauce
82   Soy Dipping Sauce
83   Daikon Radish Dipping Sauce
84   Yogurt Chutney Dipping Sauce
85   Cilantro Mustard Dipping Sauce
86   Sweet and Sour Sauce
87   Curry Mayonnaise
88   Remoulade Sauce
89   Garlic Lemon Dipping Sauce

90 Green Mayonnaise
91 Plum Sauce
92 Danish Dill Dipping Sauce
93 Sour Cream Cilantro Dipping Sauce
94 Blueberry Dipping Sauce
95 Creamy Apple Dipping Sauce
96 Teriyaki Dipping Sauce
97 Cherry Dipping Sauce
98 Mint Sauce

GREEN GODDESS DIPPING SAUCE

This is my favorite dipping sauce for all kinds of fondue meat, fish and vegetables.

3/4 cup mayonnaise
3/4 cup sour cream
1/4 cup lemon juice
1/4 cup finely chopped fresh cilantro or parsley
2 tbs. finely minced green onion
1 1/2 tbs. finely chopped chives
2 tsp. dried tarragon
1/2 tsp. minced garlic
1 tsp. anchovy paste
salt and pepper to taste

Tarragon

In a bowl, mix together mayonnaise, sour cream and lemon juice. Stir in cilantro, onion, chives, tarragon, garlic and anchovy paste. Taste and adjust seasonings. Cover and refrigerate until ready to serve.

CUCUMBER SAUCE

This sauce works very well with meat and seafood. A touch of Tabasco Sauce can add a little spike to this simple sauce.

3/4 cup grated cucumber, seeded
3/4 cup sour cream
2 tbs. balsamic or other red wine vinegar
1/2 tsp. minced garlic
2/3 tsp. salt, or more to taste
1/2 tsp. pepper

Wrap grated cucumber in cloth and squeeze out any excess moisture. Remove from cloth, mix with sour cream, vinegar, garlic and salt in a small bowl, and stir well to combine. Taste and adjust seasoning. Cover and refrigerate until ready to use.

BÉARNAISE SAUCE

Béarnaise is similar to hollandaise sauce but with additional herbs and shallots. This sauce can be served hot or cold. Use as a dipping sauce with beef, poultry, fish and vegetables.

3 tbs. red wine vinegar (prefer balsamic)
3 tbs. Chablis or other dry white wine
1 tbs. minced shallots
1/2 tsp. dried tarragon
1/2 tsp. dried chervil
1/4 tsp. white pepper

3 egg yolks
2 tbs. water
1 tsp. lemon juice
1/2 cup butter, melted
1/4 cup finely chopped fresh parsley
salt to taste

Place vinegar, wine, shallots, tarragon, chervil and white pepper in a small saucepan, and simmer until moisture is absorbed. With a food processor or blender, beat egg yolks, water and lemon juice together. With food processor blades spinning, very slowly pour hot butter into egg mixture. Process until mixture is thickened. Add parsley and salt to taste.

DIJON MUSTARD SAUCE

Makes ³/₄ cup

This is an incredibly simple sauce that can be used with almost all fried or boiled fondues. Stir in a teaspoon of finely chopped parsley if you wish to add a little color.

¹/₄ cup Dijon mustard
¹/₂ cup mayonnaise
pepper to taste

Mix mustard, mayonnaise and pepper together in a bowl. Cover and refrigerate until ready to serve.

SOUR CREAM HORSERADISH SAUCE

Makes 1 cup

This is an easy-to-prepare sauce which goes with most meats including beef, pork, veal and wild game.

2 tbs. prepared horseradish sauce, or more to taste
1 cup sour cream
1/4 tsp. dry mustard
dash of Worcestershire sauce
salt and white pepper to taste

In a bowl, mix horseradish, sour cream, mustard and Worcestershire sauce. Taste and adjust seasonings. Cover and refrigerate until ready to serve.

PARSLEY DIPPING SAUCE

This is a piquant sauce that goes with all types of meats and vegetables.

1 bunch fresh parsley, stems removed
1/2 cup olive oil
2 tbs. balsamic or other red wine vinegar
1 tsp. minced garlic
1 tsp. anchovy paste
1 pinch black pepper
1 1/2 tbs. small capers

With a food processor or blender, finely chop parsley. Add olive oil, vinegar, garlic, anchovy paste and pepper; process until well blended. Stir in capers and serve at room temperature.

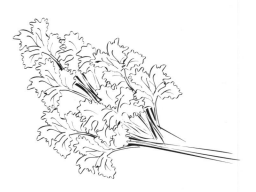

CILANTRO PEANUT SAUCE

Makes 2 cups

This flavorful sauce goes well with plain or marinated poultry, beef, pork and vegetables.

$1/2$ bunch cilantro
$1/4$–$1/2$ cup water, to taste
$1/4$ cup sugar
$1/4$ cup lemon juice
$2/3$ cup light soy sauce
$1/4$ cup rice vinegar
$1/3$ cup roasted sesame oil
1–2 tsp. minced garlic, to taste
$1/2$–$1 1/2$ tsp. red pepper flakes, to taste
$3/4$ cup chunky peanut butter

Remove stems from cilantro and finely chop leaves in a food processor work-bowl or blender container. Add water (using $1/4$ cup to start), sugar, lemon, soy, vinegar and sesame oil; adjust seasonings to taste. If you prefer a thinner sauce, add the remaining $1/4$ cup water.

SOY DIPPING SAUCE

This is an excellent sauce for tempura, as well as chicken and beef. Mirin is a sweet cooking rice wine available in the Asian foods section of most major grocery stores.

1 cup light soy sauce
1 cup mirin rice wine
1 tsp. finely minced fresh ginger, or ½ tsp. ground
   ginger

In a bowl, combine soy sauce, mirin and ginger. Chill until ready to serve.

DAIKON RADISH DIPPING SAUCE

The daikon radish adds real dimension to this sauce. Serve with tempura, or any fried fish and vegetables. Daikon radish is a long, white tuber which can be found in most large-chain grocery stores or in Asian markets. In a pinch, you could substitute red radish.

1 cup chicken stock
1/2 cup light soy sauce
1/2 cup sweet sherry or sake
pinch sugar
1–2 tbs. grated daikon radish, to taste
2 tsp. grated fresh ginger, or to taste

In a bowl or food processor workbowl, blend all ingredients together. Cover and refrigerate until ready to serve.

Note: This sauce may be served either hot or cold.

YOGURT CHUTNEY DIPPING SAUCE

Chutney is both a condiment and a sauce, usually made from mangoes and highly spiced. This dip goes well with curried meats, poultry, seafood and vegetables.

1 cup plain yogurt
½ cup mango chutney
1 tbs. finely chopped green onion

In a bowl, mix together yogurt, chutney and onion. Cover and refrigerate until ready to use.

CILANTRO MUSTARD DIPPING SAUCE

This is an excellent dip for beef and poultry. If cilantro is too strong a taste for your palate, partially substitute chopped parsley.

1 cup mayonnaise
1/3 cup finely chopped cilantro, without stems
2 tbs. Dijon mustard
1 tsp. toasted sesame oil

In a bowl, mix mayonnaise, cilantro, mustard and sesame oil. Cover and refrigerate until ready to use.

SWEET AND SOUR SAUCE

Makes 3 cups

This is a popular sauce which can be served with cooked fish, meat or vegetables. It goes especially well with battered shrimp or pork.

1 cup pineapple juice
3 tbs. ketchup
1 cup water
¼ cup sugar
3½ tbs. apple cider vinegar
½ tsp. salt
½ tbs. light soy sauce
¼ cup cornstarch
½ cup cold water

Place pineapple juice, ketchup, 1 cup water, sugar, vinegar, salt and soy sauce in a heavy saucepan, and bring to a boil, stirring well. Mix cornstarch with ½ cup cold water and stir into pineapple mixture until sauce thickens and becomes translucent. Taste and adjust flavor by adding more sugar or vinegar. Transfer mixture into a fondue pot and keep warm over low heat.

CURRY MAYONNAISE

The flavor of curry is absolutely loved by some and strongly disliked by others. This sauce goes well with curry marinated meats, plain meat, poultry, fish and vegetables.

1½ cups mayonnaise
¼ cup milk
3-4 tsp. curry powder
½ tsp. Tabasco Sauce
2 green onions, finely minced

In a mixer or food processor workbowl, blend together all ingredients. Taste and add more curry and Tabasco Sauce if desired.

REMOULADE SAUCE

Makes 1 1/2 cup

This is a spicy, piquant sauce which goes well with beef, pork, poultry and vegetables. It also goes well with cold meats.

1 cup mayonnaise
2 tbs. chopped capers
1 tbs. lemon juice
2 tsp. Dijon mustard
2 tsp. minced fresh parsley
2 tsp. chopped chives
3/4–1 tsp. anchovy paste, to taste
pepper to taste, optional

Mix all ingredients in a bowl. Taste and adjust seasonings as desired. Cover and refrigerate until ready to serve.

GARLIC LEMON DIP

This is an excellent dip for all types of seafood, beef, pork and vegetables, especially potatoes.

1 1/2 cups mayonnaise
1 tbs. minced garlic, or more to taste
1 1/2 tbs. lemon juice
1/2 tsp. cayenne pepper, or a few drops Tabasco Sauce

Combine mayonnaise, garlic, lemon juice and cayenne in a bowl. Taste and adjust seasonings. Cover and refrigerate until ready to use.

GREEN MAYONNAISE

This is an excellent sauce for fried foods like tempura, especially seafood tempura. This recipe can also be used as a dip for raw vegetables.

1/2 cup frozen spinach
2 tbs. finely chopped chives
1 1/2 tbs. chopped fresh parsley
1 tsp. dried dill weed
1 cup mayonnaise

Thaw spinach and squeeze out excess water. With a food processor or blender, process spinach, chives, parsley and dill weed into a puree. Add mayonnaise and blend until smooth. Cover and refrigerate until ready to serve.

PLUM SAUCE

Plum sauce is a thick Chinese condiment that is dark amber in color, with a sweet-tart, slightly hot flavor. It's a great sauce for pork and poultry, especially duck.

1 cup plum or apricot jam
1 tbs. dry mustard
1 tbs. cider vinegar
1/4 tsp. minced garlic
1 tsp. grated fresh ginger
1/2 tsp. soy sauce
1 pinch salt
1 pinch red pepper flakes

Place all ingredients in a saucepan and cook over medium heat until mixture begins to bubble. Taste and adjust seasonings. Allow mixture to cool before serving.

DANISH DILL DIPPING SAUCE

Try this dip flavored with Danish blue cheese. It works well with seafood, poultry and assorted vegetables.

1 1/3 cups half-and-half
1 1/3 cups dry white wine
4 egg yolks
1/2 lb. Danish blue cheese, crumbled
3/4–1 1/4 tsp. dried dill weed, or to taste

In a heavy saucepan or double boiler, whisk together half-and-half and wine, and add egg yolks and blue cheese. Heat mixture over low, beating with a whisk until smooth and creamy. Remove from heat and stir in dill weed. Cover and refrigerate until ready to serve.

SOUR CREAM CILANTRO DIPPING SAUCE

Makes 2½ cups

Cilantro is a pungent herb often used in Latin American and Asian cooking. It is much stronger than parsley with a slight musky flavor. Serve this dip with poultry, beef, pork and vegetables.

1½ cups sour cream
¾ cup mayonnaise
⅓ cup finely minced cilantro
1½ tbs. Dijon mustard
salt and pepper to taste, optional

With a food processor or blender, combine sour cream, mayonnaise, cilantro and mustard. Taste and determine if you wish to add salt and pepper. Cover and refrigerate until ready to use.

BLUEBERRY DIPPING SAUCE

This is a simple sauce which goes well with fried cheese, poultry and pork. Huckleberries can be substituted for blueberries but you may need to increase the sugar.

1 pkg. (12 oz.) frozen blueberries, thawed
1/3 cup sugar, or more to taste
1 tbs. cornstarch
1/2 cup water
1 tbs. lemon juice
1 pinch nutmeg or mace

Place blueberries and sugar in a saucepan. Mix cornstarch with water; stir into blueberry mixture with lemon juice and nutmeg. Simmer, stirring frequently, until mixture thickens. Taste and add more sugar or nutmeg if desired.

CREAMY APPLE DIPPING SAUCE

Makes 2 cups

This Swedish dip is a good accompaniment to goose and other poultry, pork and beef. Traditionally this dip is also served with sliced cold smoked meats.

$\frac{1}{2}$ lb. tart-sweet apples (Newton, Pippin, Granny Smith, or Cortland)
$\frac{1}{4}$ cup dry white wine
1 cup mayonnaise
1 tsp. horseradish sauce, or to taste
salt and pepper to taste

Pare, core and cut apples into small chunks and place in a saucepan with wine. Cover and cook over medium-low heat until apples are soft, about 15 minutes. Place in a food processor workbowl or blender container and mix until pureed. Cool pureed apples to room temperature. In a bowl, combine mayonnaise and horseradish sauce, and stir into pureed apples. Add salt and pepper to taste. Cover and refrigerate until ready to serve.

TERIYAKI DIPPING SAUCE

Teriyaki sauce is extremely popular with children and adults. Serve as an accompaniment to beef, chicken, pork and fish. Use ginger instead of garlic for variety.

⅔ cup soy sauce
⅓ cup mirin (sweet cooking rice wine)
⅓ cup sake rice wine
1 tsp. minced garlic, or ½ tsp. ground ginger
sugar to taste

Mix soy, mirin, sake and garlic in a bowl. Taste and determine if you want to add sugar. Cover and refrigerate until ready to use.

CHERRY DIPPING SAUCE

This sweet sauce can be served cold for dipping meats or hot as a dessert fondue. As a dessert fondue, try adding a cup of sliced strawberries.

1 can (29 oz.) dark sweet cherries, pitted
1 1/2 tbs. lemon juice
1 tbs. grated lemon zest
1 1/2 tbs. cornstarch
3 tbs. water
sugar to taste, optional
3 tbs. cherry liqueur, or to taste

Drain cherries and reserve juice. In a saucepan, stir cherry juice, lemon juice and lemon zest, and simmer. In a separate small bowl, mix cornstarch and water together; stir into juices. Cook on low heat until mixture thickens and turns translucent, about 10 minutes. Taste and determine if you want to add sugar. If so, cook a few minutes longer to melt sugar. Remove from heat and add liqueur to taste.

MINT SAUCE

This easy sauce is a must if serving lamb. It also goes well with poultry and pork.

1/4 cup mint leaves, without stems
2 tbs. superfine sugar
2 tbs. boiling water
1/2 cup balsamic or other red wine vinegar

Wash and dry mint leaves. Mix chopped leaves and sugar together on a cutting board and finely mince. Put mixture into a bowl and pour boiling water over. Stir until sugar dissolves. Cool to room temperature and add vinegar. Taste and determine if you wish to add more sugar or vinegar.

DESSERT FONDUES

100   Caramel Fondue
101   Classic Chocolate Fondue
102   Coconut-Caramel Dessert Fondue
103   Sesame Seed Custard
104   White Chocolate Amaretto Fondue
105   Cookies and Cream Marshmallow Dip
106   Milk Chocolate Irish Cream
107   Ebony and Ivory Dessert Fondue
108   Ginger Cream
109   Raisin Rum Fondue
110   Hazelnut Dessert Fondue
111   Creamy Cherry Fondue
112   Creamy Mocha Fondue
113   Butterscotch Fondue
114   Maple Walnut Fondue
115   Candied Fruit Fritters
116   Peanut Butter Fondue
117   Fruit Custard Fondue
118   Almond Fruit Fondue

CARAMEL FONDUE

Caramel is a very popular flavor for fondue, as for other desserts. You can substitute 2-3 tbs. dark rum or 1-2 tsp. rum extract for the vanilla. Serve with fresh fruit (especially apples and bananas), angel food cake, chocolate cookies and/or pound cake.

1 cup sugar
2 cups cream
2 tsp. vanilla or rum extract
1 cup chopped, toasted pecans or almonds, optional

In a heavy saucepan, heat sugar over medium-high heat until sugar is melted and light brown in color, about 3 to 4 minutes. Shake and tilt pan to move sugar around until proper color is achieved. Be very careful not to scorch.

Remove pan from heat; pour in cream and vanilla or rum extract. Return pan to heat and stir until smooth. Boil, stirring occasionally until mixture thickens and coats the back of a spoon, about 10 minutes. Transfer thickened caramel to fondue pot and keep warm over low heat.

CLASSIC CHOCOLATE FONDUE

Servings: 4

For best results, use the best chocolate you can find. Serve with strawberries, banana, pears or apples. Or try serving with cubes of pound cake, angel food cake and miniature cream puffs.

1 cup whipping cream
2²/₃ cup finely chopped semi-sweet chocolate
2 tsp. vanilla extract
2 tbs. dark rum or other liqueur (Amaretto, Frangelico or Grand Marnier), optional

In a saucepan, slowly heat whipping cream until bubbles form around edge. Remove pan from heat; whisk in chopped chocolate until mixture is smooth. Stir in vanilla and, if desired, add rum or liqueur of choice. Transfer mixture to a fondue pot and keep warm over low heat.

Note: For fruits that darken, such as pears and apples, drizzle a few drops of lemon juice on the cut fruit.

COCONUT-CARAMEL DESSERT FONDUE

Servings: 6-8

This great dessert would be good served with cubes of chocolate cake, miniature cream puffs, cubed nut breads or fresh fruit. You can add texture to this recipe by garnishing with 1 cup toasted coconut or finely chopped toasted walnuts.

2/3 cup sugar
3 cups half-and-half
1 cup coconut milk
1/4 cup cream of coconut

4 eggs
6 tbs. sugar
1 tsp. cinnamon

In a heavy saucepan, cook 2/3 cup sugar over medium-high heat until sugar melts and turns a caramel color; gently swirl pan to distribute sugar evenly. Remove pan from heat and carefully stir in 1 cup of the half-and-half. Return pan to stove and cook on low heat, stirring until caramel is dissolved, and set aside.

In another saucepan, heat remaining 2 cups half-and-half, coconut milk and coconut cream over low heat. In a separate bowl, beat eggs with 6 tbs. sugar and slowly whisk in warmed milk mixture; add caramel mixture. Transfer back to a heavy saucepan; cook over medium-low heat until mixture thickens to the consistency of custard, about 5 minutes. Transfer to a fondue pot and keep warm over low heat.

SESAME SEED CUSTARD

This is a wonderful almond-flavored, thick egg custard, fried and dipped in sweetened sesame seeds.

4 eggs, beaten
1 cup flour
6 tbs. cornstarch
1 1/2 cups cold water
2 tbs. sugar

1 1/2–2 tbs. pure almond extract
1/2 cup cornstarch for coating
1/2 cup toasted sesame seeds
1/2 cup superfine sugar

In a bowl, combine eggs, flour and 6 tbs. cornstarch. Add 1 cup of the water, a little at a time, until mixture is smooth. In a saucepan, bring remaining 1/2 cup water to a boil; add egg mixture and 2 tbs. sugar. Reduce heat to low; stir constantly until mixture becomes firm, about 10 minutes. Stir in almond extract and remove from heat. Pour mixture into a greased 8-inch baking pan and smooth surface with a spatula. Cool, cover and refrigerate for 2 to 3 hours. Cut custard into small rectangles and roll in cornstarch. Cook in hot oil until golden brown. Mix sesame seeds with superfine sugar and serve in a bowl for immediate dipping after cooking custard.

WHITE CHOCOLATE AMARETTO FONDUE

Serve with an assortment of fresh fruit, shortbread cookies, brownies and/or pound cake. Consider changing the liqueur to Frangelico and using chopped toasted hazelnuts instead of almonds.

12 oz. white chocolate, grated
1 cup whipping cream
2 tbs. amaretto liqueur, or more to taste
1/2 cup toasted chopped almonds, optional

In a double boiler, slowly heat white chocolate and cream, stirring constantly. When chocolate is completely melted and smooth, stir in liqueur to taste. If desired, stir in toasted nuts.

COOKIES AND CREAM MARSHMALLOW DREAM Servings: 4-6

This is a very rich and creamy fondue, especially popular with kids. Serve with bananas, cheesecake squares, pound cake and, of course, Oreos.

12 oz. semi-sweet chocolate, grated
1 cup whipping cream
1 cup marshmallow cream
2 tbs. chocolate liqueur, or other liqueur, optional
1/2–1 cup crushed Oreo cookies, to taste

In a saucepan, heat chocolate and cream over low until melted and smooth, stirring constantly. Spoon marshmallow cream on top of chocolate. Use a blowtorch or a broiler to lightly brown marshmallow cream. Gently stir in browned marshmallow. Taste and determine if you wish to add liqueur, and sprinkle the top with Oreo cookies. Keep warm over low heat.

MILK CHOCOLATE IRISH CREAM

This is a mild, creamy fondue that goes well with cake, miniature cream puffs, fruit and/or crisp cookies.

12 oz. milk chocolate, grated
1 cup whipping cream
2–3 tbs. Bailey's Irish Cream, to taste

In a saucepan or fondue pot, slowly heat milk chocolate and cream, stirring constantly. When chocolate is completely melted and smooth, stir in Bailey's Irish Cream. Taste and adjust the amount of liqueur.

EBONY AND IVORY DESSERT FONDUE

Swirl dark chocolate with white chocolate and you have an impressive dessert fondue. I like to serve a bowl of chopped toasted nuts (pecans, walnuts or peanuts) alongside to coat the dipped fruit or cake.

12 oz. semi-sweet or dark chocolate, grated
1 1/2 cups whipping cream
2 tbs. liqueur of choice (orange curacao, crème de menthe, Frangelico, amaretto, or other)
12 oz. white chocolate, grated
1 1/2 tsp. vanilla extract, or liqueur of choice

In a small saucepan, stir together semi-sweet chocolate and 1 cup of the cream over low heat until smooth. Add liqueur of choice to taste. In a double boiler, heat white chocolate and remaining 1/2 cup cream; stir until smooth. Stir in vanilla or liqueur of choice. Pour dark chocolate mixture into a fondue pot and spoon dollops of white chocolate mixture on top. Using a knife, gently swirl chocolate mixtures together, using a figure-8 motion. Keep fondue warm over low heat.

GINGER CREAM

This is a subtle creamy fondue that does not use chocolate. Serve assorted fruits, chocolate cake, cookies and/or brownies as an accompaniment.

8 thick slices fresh ginger
2 cups half-and-half
6 egg yolks
1/3 cup sugar

In a heavy saucepan, simmer ginger and half-and-half together for 10 minutes to infuse cream with ginger flavor. In a mixer, beat egg yolks with sugar until egg mixture turns pale yellow. Slowly pour ginger mixture into egg mixture. Transfer sauce back to saucepan; cook on medium-low heat until mixture thickens, stirring constantly. Pour sauce into a sieve to remove ginger and any lumps. Transfer mixture into a fondue pot and keep warm over low heat. If you desire a more intense ginger flavor, add a pinch of ground ginger.

RAISIN RUM FONDUE

Serve with angel food cake, pound cake, bananas and/or spice cake. This can also be used as a sauce for ice cream or bread pudding.

2 1/2 cups heavy cream
10 tbs. sugar
2 tbs. cornstarch
1/4 cup cold milk
2/3 cup dark rum, or to taste
1/3 cup golden raisins
1 pinch cinnamon, optional

Place cream and sugar in a heavy saucepan and bring to a boil. Mix cornstarch and milk together and stir into cream mixture. Reduce heat to a simmer and cook until mixture thickens, about 2 minutes. Add rum and raisins and simmer for 2 minutes. Taste and determine if you wish to add cinnamon. Transfer to a fondue pot and keep warm over low heat.

HAZELNUT DESSERT FONDUE

Serve this with assorted fruit, angel food cake chunks, pound cake, cheesecake bites, or doughnuts. Some people do not like nuts, so serve them in a bowl alongside for dipping.

2½ cups whipping cream
2½ tbs. cornstarch
¼ cup sugar
6 tbs. Frangelico hazelnut liqueur
½–¾ cup chopped toasted hazelnuts, to taste

Mix cream, cornstarch and sugar together in a small saucepan. Cook on medium heat until smooth and thick. Stir in liqueur and hazelnuts. Transfer to a fondue pot and keep warm over low heat.

CREAMY CHERRY FONDUE

Servings: 4

This is a great sauce for dipping vanilla, chocolate and/or cherry pound cake pieces. It is also good with angel food cake, meringue cookies, or served over ice cream. If you prefer a nonalcoholic version, use 1–2 tsp. cherry or almond extract in place of liqueur.

2 cans (16 oz. each) pitted cherries, with juice
1 cup whipping cream
$1/2$ cup sugar, or to taste
$1/4$ cup cornstarch
3–4 tbs. cherry liqueur or brandy, to taste

Place cherries and their juice in a blender container; process until cherries are coarsely chopped. Pour cherries into a saucepan with cream, sugar and cornstarch. Cook on medium heat until mixture thickens. Stir in liqueur, taste, and determine if you wish to add more. Transfer mixture to a fondue pot and keep warm.

CREAMY MOCHA FONDUE

What could be more appealing to caffeine lovers than a blend of chocolate and coffee. Serve with cake, angel food cake, cookies, miniature cream puffs and bananas.

6 egg yolks
2/3 cup sugar
2 cups half-and-half
2 tbs. instant coffee powder
2 oz. semi-sweet or bittersweet dark chocolate, melted

With a food processor or blender, process egg yolks and 1/3 cup of the sugar until mixture turns a pale yellow. Place half-and-half, remaining 1/3 cup sugar and coffee powder in a saucepan and bring to a boil. Remove from heat and pour coffee mixture slowly into egg mixture, whisking constantly until smooth. Return to saucepan and cook on medium heat, stirring with a wooden spoon until mixture thickens and coats the spoon. Stir in melted chocolate. Transfer mixture to a fondue pot and keep warm over low heat.

BUTTERSCOTCH FONDUE

It is important to use light brown sugar to create the proper butterscotch color. Serve with angel food cake, pound cake, miniature cream puffs, doughnuts, marshmallows and assorted fruits. Serve a bowl of chopped toasted nuts for a second dip.

1 cup unsalted butter
2 cups light brown sugar, packed
1 cup cream
6 tbs. light corn syrup
few drops lemon juice

In a heavy saucepan, melt butter, and add brown sugar, cream, corn syrup and lemon juice. Bring to a boil, reduce heat and simmer for 5 minutes. Transfer mixture to a fondue pot and keep warm over low heat.

MAPLE WALNUT FONDUE

This is a delightful concoction which can also serve as a topping for ice cream. If mixture begins to thicken while simmering in the fondue pot, thin with a little pure maple syrup. Serve with pound cake, bananas, miniature cream puffs and/or angel food cake.

12 oz. white chocolate, grated
1 cup cream
1–2 tbs. pure maple extract, to taste
1 pinch cinnamon
1/2 cup chopped toasted walnuts

In a double boiler, heat white chocolate and cream on low heat, stirring constantly, until mixture is smooth and creamy. Add maple extract and cinnamon to taste. Stir in walnuts, transfer mixture to a fondue pot and keep warm over low heat.

CANDIED FRUIT FRITTERS

For this treat, fruit is battered, cooked in oil, covered with a glaze and dipped in ice water to form a hard shell. Cooked yams or sweet potatoes can be substituted for the fruit.

6 tbs. flour
6 tbs. cornstarch
2 tbs. cold water
2 eggs, beaten
3 bananas or apples

oil for deep fat frying
2 tbs. vegetable oil
$3/4$ cup sugar
1–2 tbs. sesame seeds

In a bowl, mix flour, cornstarch, water and eggs. Cut bananas into 1-inch chunks; or pare, core and cut apples into thick wedges. Dip fruit in batter and cook in hot oil until golden brown, about $1\frac{1}{2}$ to 2 minutes. In a saucepan, heat oil and sugar on medium heat until sugar turns a light golden brown color; add sesame seeds. Keep this sauce warm for dipping. Place a bowl of ice water next to sugar glaze. Dip fried fruit in glaze and immediately dip in ice water.

PEANUT BUTTER FONDUE

This is a favorite of peanut butter lovers, of course! Serve with chunks of bananas and apples, chocolate pound cake, crisp cookies (especially Oreos), angel food cake and/or doughnuts.

2 cups (12 oz.) grated white chocolate
¾ cup smooth or chunky peanut butter
1 cup cream

Melt white chocolate in a double boiler. Stir in peanut butter until well mixed—use chunky peanut butter if you like extra texture. Slowly stir in cream. Taste and add more peanut butter if desired. Transfer to a fondue pot and keep warm over low heat. Mixture will thicken as it cooks. If you wish to thin it, add a little warmed cream.

FRUIT CUSTARD FONDUE

This fondue is perfect for dipping fresh fruit, angel food cake or pound cake. If you have leftovers, chill the custard and use it as a dressing for fruit salad. You can substitute canned or fresh peaches or nectarines for the berries—just puree in a blender container or food processor workbowl first.

1/4 cup butter
1 cup sugar
3 large eggs
1 cup milk, scalded
1 tsp. vanilla extract
1 pinch nutmeg or mace
1 cup crushed berries (raspberries, blackberries or loganberries)

With a mixer, beat butter and sugar together until fluffy. Add eggs and beat well. Add scalded milk and mix well. Pour into a double boiler and cook until custard thickens. Add vanilla, nutmeg and crushed berries. Taste and add more nutmeg if desired. Strain mixture through a sieve to remove seeds. Transfer mixture to a fondue pot. Keep warm over low heat.

ALMOND FRUIT FONDUE

The unusual ingredient in this spicy dessert fondue is curry. It goes best with tropical fruit like pineapple, mangoes, papayas, melons and bananas. For added flavor, toast the coconut.

1 cup chicken broth
1 cup dry white wine
2 tsp. curry powder, or more to taste
1/4 cup water
1 1/2 tbs. quick-cooking tapioca
1 tsp. sugar, or more to taste
1 cup slivered almonds, toasted
1 cup coconut
1/2 cup golden raisins

In a saucepan, combine broth, wine and curry powder and simmer for 30 minutes. In a bowl, combine water, tapioca and sugar and soak for 5 minutes. Add tapioca mixture to broth mixture and stir until thickened. Add almonds, coconut and raisins. Stir to combine; taste and determine if you wish to add more sugar. Transfer mixture to a fondue pot and keep warm over low heat.

INDEX

A

Almond fruit fondue 118
Anchovy dip, Italian 33
Apple dipping sauce, creamy 95
Apricot sauce 34
Artichoke and green chile dip 37

B

Bacon and Danish cheese fondue 14
Barbecue dip, hot 28
Basil marinara dip 30
Bean and beef dip 41
Bean dip, hot 38
Bearnaise sauce 77
Beef
    and bean dip 41
    beer-marinated, for hot oil or broth fondue 59
    cheddar fondue, easy 20
    corned, dip 27
    double dip meatballs, for oil fondue 53
    ginger, for oil or broth fondue 51
    marinated steak, for oil or broth fondue 52
    quick and easy, for oil or broth fondue 46
    stock 65
    sukiyaki dinner 68
Beer-marinated beef, for hot oil or broth fondue 59
Blackberry dip, savory 31
Blueberry dipping sauce 94
Brie cheese, creamy 13
Broths, cooking
    beef stock 65
    coq au vin 62
    court bouillon 63
    fish stock 64
    French onion 72
    Madeira 70
    mushroom 71
    Oriental 61
    saffron 69
    sukiyaki 67
    wine 66
Buttermilk fondue 21
Butterscotch fondue 113

C

Caramel fondue 1001
Caramel-coconut dessert fondue 102
Cheddar beef fondue, easy 20
Cheese (see also Cheese fondues)
    feta, and cilantro dip 36
    fried, for oil fondue 47
    Gorgonzola dip 39
Cheese fondues
    and chicken 17
    buttermilk 21
    caramelized onion 8
    chili 22
    creamy Brie 13
    creamy shrimp 16
    Danish cheese and bacon 14
    Dutch 7
    easy cheddar beef 20
    fiesta 11
    green chile 10
    Mediterranean 12
    nonalcoholic 15
    smoked 9
    Stilton 19
    Swiss cheese and egg 18

Cherry
    dipping sauce 97
    fondue, creamy 111
    -marinated chicken, for oil or
       broth fondue 57
Chicken
    Asian, for oil or broth fondue
       44
    and cheese fondue 17
    cherry-marinated,for hot oil or
       broth fondue 57
    coconut, for hot oil fondue 58
    slices, tender, for oil fondue 49
    tenders, spicy, for oil fondue
       55
Chile, green, and artichoke dip 37
Chile, green, fondue 10
Chili fondue 22
Chocolate
    ebony and ivory dessert fondue
       107
    fondue, classic 101
    milk, Irish cream 106
Chutney yogurt dipping sauce 84
Cilantro
    and feta cheese dip 36
    mustard dipping sauce 85

peanut sauce 81
    sour cream dipping sauce 93
Clam dip, hot 29
Coconut-caramel dessert fondue
    102
Cookies and cream marshmallow
    dream 105
Coq au vin cooking broth 62
Corned beef dip 27
Court bouillon 63
Crab dip 25
Cucumber sauce 76
Curry dip, red 32
Curry mayonnaise 87
Custard, fruit, fondue 117
Custard, sesame seed 103

D

Daikon radish dipping sauce 83
Danish cheese and bacon fondue
    14
Danish dill dipping sauce 92
Dessert fondues
    almond fruit 118
    butterscotch 113
    candied fruit fritters 115
    caramel 100

classic chocolate 101
coconut-caramel 102
cookies and cream marshmal-
    low dream 105
creamy cherry 111
creamy mocha 112
ebony and ivory 107
fruit custard 117
ginger cream 108
hazelnut 110
maple walnut 114
milk chocolate Irish cream 106
peanut butter 116
raisin rum fondue 109
sesame seed custard 103
white chocolate amaretto 104
Dijon mustard sauce 78
Dill dipping sauce, Danish 92
Dipping sauces
    bearnaise 77
    blueberry 94
    cherry 97
    cilantro mustard 85
    cilantro peanut 81
    creamy apple 95
    cucumber 76
    curry mayonnaise 87

Dipping sauces *continued*
    daikon radish 83
    Danish dill 92
    Dijon mustard 78
    garlic lemon 89
    Green Goddess 75
    green mayonnaise 90
    mint 98
    parsley 80
    plum 91
    remoulade 88
    sour cream cilantro 93
    sour cream horseradish 79
    soy 82
    sweet and sour 86
    teriyaki 96
    yogurt chutney 84
Dips, hot
    apricot sauce 34
    basil marinara 30
    beef and bean 41
    corned beef 27
    crab 25
    feta cheese and cilantro 36
    Gorgonzola 39
    green chile and artichoke 37
    hot barbecue 28
    hot bean 38
    hot clam 29
    hot shrimp and mushroom 35
    hot spinach 40
    Italian anchovy 33
    Marsala tomato 24
    pecan sour cream 42
    red curry 32
    sausage mushroom 26
    savory blackberry 31
Dutch cheese fondue 7

E
Ebony and ivory dessert fondue
    107

F
Feta cheese and cilantro dip 36
Fiesta cheese fondue 11
Fish, battered, for oil fondue 54
Fish stock 64
Fondue
    cooking temperatures 5
    do's and don'ts 1-3
    equipment 3-5
Fritters, candied fruit 115

Fruit
    almond fondue 118
    apricot sauce 34
    blueberry dipping sauce 94
    cherry dipping sauce 97
    creamy apple dipping sauce 95
    creamy cherry fondue 111
    custard fondue 117
    fritters, candied, for oil fondue
      115
    plum sauce 91
    savory blackberry dip 31

G
Garlic lemon dipping sauce 89
Ginger beef, for oil or broth fondue
    51
Ginger cream 108
Gorgonzola dip 39
Green Goddess dipping sauce 75
Green mayonnaise 90

H
Hazelnut dessert fondue 110
Horseradish sour cream sauce 79

I

Italian anchovy dip 33

L

Lamb, marinated, for oil or broth fondue 45

Lamb, merlot, for oil or broth fondue 56

Lemon garlic dipping sauce 89

M

Madeira broth 70

Maple walnut fondue 114

Marinara basil dip 30

Marsala tomato dip 24

Mayonnaise, curry 87

Mayonnaise, green 90

Meatballs, double dip, for oil fondue 53

Mediterranean fondue 12

Merlot lamb, for hot oil or broth fondue 56

Mint sauce 98

Mocha fondue, creamy 112

Mushroom
   broth 71
   sausage dip 26

and shrimp dip, hot 35

Mustard cilantro dipping sauce 85

N

Nonalcoholic cheese fondue 15

O

Oil fondues (see also Oil or broth fondues)
   battered fish 54
   coconut chicken 58
   double dip meatballs 53
   fried cheese 47
   prawn balls 50
   shrimp and vegetable tempura 48
   spicy chicken tenders 55
   tender chicken slices 49

Oil or broth fondues
   Asian chicken 44
   beer-marinated beef 59
   cherry-marinated chicken 57
   ginger beef 51
   marinated lamb 45
   marinated steak 52
   merlot lamb 56
   quick and easy beef 46

Onion broth, French 72

Onion, caramelized, fondue 8

Oriental cooking broth 61

P

Parsley dipping sauce 80

Peanut butter fondue 116

Peanut cilantro sauce 81

Pecan sour cream dip 42

Plum sauce 91

Prawn balls, for oil fondue 50

R

Raisin rum fondue 109

Red curry dip 32

Remoulade sauce 88

Rum raisin fondue 109

S

Saffron broth 69

Sausage mushroom dip 26

Savory blackberry dip 31

Seafood
   battered fish, for oil fondue 54
   crab dip 25
   creamy shrimp fondue 16
   fish stock 64

Dipping sauces *continued*
    hot clam dip 29
    hot shrimp and mushroom dip 35
    Italian anchovy dip 33
    prawn balls, for oil fondue 50
Sesame seed custard, for oil fondue 103
Shrimp
    fondue, creamy 16
    and mushroom dip, hot 35
    and vegetable tempura 48
Smoked cheese fondue 9
Sour cream
    cilantro dipping sauce 93
    horseradish sauce 79
    pecan dip 42
Soy dipping sauce 82
Spinach dip, hot 40
Steak, marinated, for oil or broth fondue 52
Stilton cheese fondue 19
Sukiyaki broth 67
Sukiyaki dinner 68
Sweet and sour sauce 86
Swiss cheese and egg fondue 18

T
Teriyaki dipping sauce 96
Tomato Marsala dip 24

V
Vegetable and shrimp tempura 48

W
Walnut maple fondue 114
White chocolate amaretto fondue 104
Wine cooking broth 66

Y
Yogurt chutney dipping sauce 84

Serve Creative, Easy, Nutritious Meals with nitty gritty® Cookbooks

100 Dynamite Desserts
The 9 x 13 Pan Cookbook
The Barbecue Cookbook
Beer and Good Food
The Best Bagels are Made at Home
The Best Pizza is Made at Home
The Big Book of Bread Machine
  Recipes
Bread Baking
Bread Machine Cookbook
Bread Machine Cookbook II
Bread Machine Cookbook III
Bread Machine Cookbook IV
Bread Machine Cookbook V
Bread Machine Cookbook VI
Cappuccino/Espresso
Casseroles
The Coffee Book
Convection Oven Cookery
The Cook-Ahead Cookbook
Cooking for 1 or 2
Cooking in Clay
Cooking in Porcelain

Cooking on the Indoor Grill
Cooking with Chile Peppers
Cooking with Grains
Cooking with Your Kids
The Dehydrator Cookbook
Edible Pockets for Every Meal
Extra-Special Crockery Pot Recipes
Fabulous Fiber Cookery
Fondue and Hot Dips
Fresh Vegetables
From Freezer, 'Fridge and Pantry
From Your Ice Cream Maker
The Garlic Cookbook
Gourmet Gifts
Healthy Cooking on the Run
Healthy Snacks for Kids
The Juicer Book
The Juicer Book II
Lowfat American Favorites
New International Fondue Cookbook
No Salt, No Sugar, No Fat
One-Dish Meals
The Pasta Machine Cookbook

Pinch of Time: Meals in Less than 30
  Minutes
Quick and Easy Pasta Recipes
Recipes for the Loaf Pan
Recipes for the Pressure Cooker
Recipes for Yogurt Cheese
Risottos, Paellas, and other Rice
  Specialties
Rotisserie Oven Cooking
The Sandwich Maker Cookbook
The Sensational Skillet: Sautés and
  Stir-Fries
Slow Cooking in Crock-Pot,® Slow
  Cooker, Oven and Multi-Cooker
Soups and Stews
The Toaster Oven Cookbook
Unbeatable Chicken Recipes
The Vegetarian Slow Cooker
New Waffles and Pizzelles
The Well Dressed Potato
Wraps and Roll-Ups

For a free catalog, call: Bristol Publishing Enterprises, Inc.
(800) 346-4889
www.bristolcookbooks.com